DEER MAN

DEER MANAGEMENT
IMPROVED HERDS FOR GREATER PROFIT

A. J. de NAHLIK

DAVID & CHARLES

NEWTON ABBOT   LONDON

NORTH POMFRET (VT)   VANCOUVER

o 7153 6548 7

Library of Congress Catalog Card Number 74 81597

© A. J. de Nahlik 1974

Set in 11 on 13 pt Garamond and printed in
Great Britain by Ebenezer Baylis & Son Limited
The Trinity Press Worcester and London
for David & Charles (Holdings) Limited
South Devon House Newton Abbot Devon

Published in the United States of America
by David & Charles Inc North Pomfret
Vermont 05053 USA

Published in Canada by Douglas David &
Charles Limited 3645 McKechnie Drive
West Vancouver BC

To Piffa and Bruno Schroder, with my sincere thanks
for their generous help and encouragement

CONTENTS

	page
Acknowledgements	11
Introduction	13

PART ONE: DEER IN THEIR ENVIRONMENT

1 Deer in Britain—History, Habitat, Habits	21
2 Body and Tooth Development as Aids to Recognition	41
3 Characteristics of Antler Development	62

PART TWO: DEER MANAGEMENT

4 Deer Counting	91
5 Deer Damage	97
6 Density	116
7 Feeding and Shelter	125
8 Planned Management	139
9 Co-operation	150

PART THREE: DEER ECONOMICS

10 General Considerations	161
11 Evaluation of Stalking	167
12 Deer as Economic Product	180

Appendices

1 Chemical Deterrents	189
2 Percentage Analysis of Fodder and Plants with Which Deer May Come into Contact in Their Habitat	193
3 The Hoffman Pyramid	198
4 Basic Planning of Deer Management for Economic Return	203
5 General Considerations of Deer Economics	212
6 Balance of Sex Ratio in Deer Economics	219

7 Sex Ratio and Culling of Calves   228
8 Other Income from Deer   237
9 Comparison of Deer and Sheep   239

References   245

Index   247

LIST OF ILLUSTRATIONS

PLATES   *page*

Fossilised roe deer antler	65
Four prehistoric roe heads	65
Prehistoric red deer head	65
Reconstruction of fossilised red deer head	65
The Endsleigh Head	66
Warnham blood head	66
Heads of father and son with inherited characteristics	66
Wear of teeth establishing age	83
Red deer recognition by 'rectangular' shape of head	84
Group of stags	84
A good 10-pointer	133
Two young stags	133
Collection of good stags	134
Stags of two age groups	134
Three good stags in velvet	151
Good fallow deer buck	151
Antlers caught in soft wire mesh fence	152
'Corkscrew' head	152

IN TEXT

Antler characteristics	34
Antler and sex development in the yearly cycle	37
Red deer recognition by body shape	43
Roe deer recognition by body build	44-5
Life cycle of a stag	49
Antler cycle of fallow deer	51
Life cycle of a buck	52
Development of lower jaw teeth, red and roe deer	54

Age estimation by incisors 56
Age estimation by wear of the third molar 57
Shape of the register in the molar tooth 58
Antler shape as a guide to recognition, red deer 63
Red deer antler development, first to fifth head 68
Red deer antler development, sixth and subsequent heads 69
Assessment of 8- and 10-pointers 72
Roe deer antler development, first and second heads, mature
and old buck 75-8
Fallow deer antler development 81-5
Individual tree protection methods 105-7
Protection of individual leading shoots 108
Browsing damage to terminal buds 111
Red deer antler measurement card 171
Fallow deer antler measurement card 173
Roe deer antler measurement card 174
Hoffman pyramid, red deer 200-1
Hoffman pyramid, roe deer 202
Weight and development of stags and hinds related to age 205
Deer population presented as a triangle 207
Triangular representation of surplus calves 207
Culling guide, related to quality and age 210
Body development in relation to age 213
Antler and fertility development in relation to age 214
Age distribution of stags and hinds shot 1968 season 216
Revenue to sex ratio relationship 222
Individual forests within group 'X' 224
Deer counted and shot in 'X' group of forests 225
Relationship between sex ratio and calving with 1,063 adult
animals 232

ACKNOWLEDGEMENTS

The preparation of this work would have been impossible if help had not been forthcoming from many sources. Private, public, government and scientific organisations and individuals have made generous contributions providing facilities for research, information, access to records and sharing of experiences gained, whilst the authors and publishers allowed the use of existing published material.

My thanks go therefore to the Nature Conservancy, Forestry Commission, Scottish Red Deer Commission, Rowett Institute and to many of their employees individually, to many deer forest owners throughout Britain and to their keepers and ghillies; in particular I am very grateful to the Lairds of Islay and their keepers, who for some years have been generous in the facilities they offered me.

Particular thanks, however, are due to a few special individuals. Firstly to my wife who has drawn most of the illustrations, changing and improving them to bring out the points which needed highlighting; to Piffa Schroder who, with remarkable devotion, edited the manuscript and formed it into readable material, and suggested many changes and improvements to the substance and appearance of the book; to Mrs Doris Morris who has typed and retyped the manuscripts, working often against the clock; and, last but not least, to Bruno Schroder who, by his interest and devotion to deer, has not only reignited my own interest in deer but focused it upon the area of economic deer management.

A. J. de N.

INTRODUCTION

It is interesting to speculate why matters connected with deer seem to generate so much argument and high feeling and, frequently, such extremely polarised viewpoints. On the other hand, it is equally interesting to find that some of these arguments cover, and therefore to some extent bind together, the furthest regions of the globe, and that such dissimilar areas as a New Zealand mountain range, a Hebridean isle and a Russian forest should be linked as passionately and irrevocably as only those parts of the world can be whose members are bound together by a sort of esoteric fraternity, like those of madmen, politicians or sportsmen. These three might be said to combine in the case of the deer-orientated community at any rate, for it could be suggested that politics flies out of the window to allow for a more important element, the 'madness of sport', to emerge; yet, as time progresses, the same devotion that once led to the slaughter of beasts and the chase now finds its natural, and inevitable, counterpart in the conservation of those beasts and their protection. For if war and hunger were the origins of the hunt, then, with their growing love of sport which turned into a pastime engendered originally by necessity, sportsmen learned to love the land and the beasts which had provided their food and their recreation.

In broad terms, deer have played their role in the life of the British Isles since time immemorial and must once have constituted a significant proportion of the population's diet. In ancient days, however, the deer were forest-dwellers, little if at all disturbed by human culture; humans were as much a part of mother nature as other living beings; but as human culture developed, the original balance of nature became upset.

It does not seem likely that the development of early agriculture conflicted with deer or vice versa. The population was small, and apart from low-level expansion and migration, the requirements for agricultural land were limited to the proximity of habitation. The latter was not in conflict with deer while agricultural land, being normally close to the dwellings, left the animals with vast tracts of land to roam freely. The first intrusion of man upon deer's habitat, mainly in Scotland, was the disappearance of forests.

It is interesting to note that the reaction of the animals, as reflected in their behaviour, where similar occurrences take place —namely where forest disappears—repeats itself. Either the deer migrate and conversely the appearance of a new forest attracts them even over a great distance (even if we do not know how the animals learn of the new forest's existence), or, where migration is impossible on account of natural obstacles, deer will adapt to the rigours of the new environment if this is at all possible.

There can be little doubt that deer living on afforested land are capable of finding food, both throughout the year and with greater ease, than deer living on open moor; in the first place, trees form a type of barrier which, under winter conditions, decreases the snow cover, either by forming a snow-bearing canopy or else by acting as a wind brake which causes snow to drift and mass in one area, leaving the earth exposed elsewhere. Even if this were not so, trees—especially the deciduous variety— produce bark, shoots and buds, all of which form a part of deer's diet. Even though it is said that the Scottish forest was originally a pine forest, it must have had a proportion of birch, larch and oak, with a layer of undergrowth which provided a diet supplement. Deprived of this easily available supply of food, the deer had to change their habits. As forest-dwellers, deer tend to feed mainly in the morning and evening, sleeping, resting and chewing cud during the remainder of the time. Their supply of food being reduced, in terms both of quality and quantity, the moorland deer have become daytime feeders purely because they had to assure themselves of the intake of food which they require for survival.

In spite of longer feeding hours, Scottish red deer suffered from the fact that their food intake, in terms of quantity and quality, had decreased, with consequent reduction in the size of the deer themselves; this is the origin of the development of a smaller species, physically adjusted to that which the new environment could support.

Whilst the situation outlined is related mainly to Scotland's red deer, there is a parallel to be found with roe deer. There are a few areas on the Continent where roe found itself in the open land almost devoid of forest. Referred to as 'field roe', they too had changed their habits. For instance, they live for most of the year in herds of 20–30 animals of mixed sexes, except for a period of a few weeks immediately before, during and after the rut. This species of roe has not changed much physically, for its habitat is rich in good-quality food produced by agriculture. Thus, whilst adaptation of different habits to environmental conditions has taken place in the case of roe described above, an adaptation of body was needed in the case of moorland deer.

Just as evolution has worked in one direction, so the reverse situation is possible, not to say logical; increased quantity and quality of food will—and does—result in development of deer in body, antler size and health.

If the first intrusion of human culture upon deer habitat was of such lasting importance to the species, so was the second: the extermination of predators. Wolves, wild cats and eagles are not common features of the countryside today. We humans have exterminated them to a greater or lesser extent for a variety of reasons; the protection of fellow humans and the conservation of farm stocks, to mention just two. Indeed so total was the elimination, that today the eagle is a 'protected' species as is the wild cat, whilst the others are beyond protection. The extermination of these animals has once again unbalanced nature as far as the deer are concerned. The role of predators in nature was to control numbers, by taking out the weak and unhealthy specimens; if one looks at the animals in those areas of the world where predators still roam the countryside, as for instance in many African countries, one finds that among the smaller animals the health factor is high and condition good. The reason for this is that the sick and suffering are taken by lions, leopards, wild dogs, hyenas, eagles and others; a similar phenomenon can be observed in some European countries where wolves and wild cats are not uncommon and are still a part of the natural environment.

Having exterminated the larger predators in Britain, or even the partial carnivora like wild pig or bear, we have failed to provide a proper substitute in relation to deer for a very long time; indeed we have played a role in opposition to that of predators, taking—for sport or food—the large, strong animals because their trophy or carcass represented the optimum value, and leaving the weak and sick to fend for themselves, to propagate if they could, spreading their ailments, or to perish slowly and possibly painfully. Some of us are prepared to go to considerable lengths and expense condemning bloodsports and complaining of cruelty through hunting, shooting or stalking; no one ever mentions the cruelty of lack of control, that much-needed control which we humans, who have exterminated the natural control by predators, have a duty to exercise in order to maintain the balance in population and health of our deer. Indeed it is the stalking sportsmen, keepers and ghillies who, in more recent years, have accepted their responsibility in this respect and have started to control selectively, restoring the balance and improving the species in health and general quality.

The most recent conflict between the human and the deer interest is that stemming from the increase in human population, and the consequent demands for food, clothing, living space and materials which increase likewise. In each case deer are affected, inasmuch as a high density of population, industrialisation and agricultural cultivation do not tolerate the apparently unproductive areas required by deer, the damage caused by deer and even the food which deer consume on the high moor or elsewhere which perhaps could be used by domestic stock.

So where do matters stand? Is there room for deer in our life and, if so, are they to be for 'decoration', for the interests of natural history, or can deer play a role in the national economy, and if so, how?

We will see that deer, if properly looked after, can play a constructive role in our life and can provide a balanced return for our effort, care and money. But to bring about that return, we have to accept the fact that there is much to be done and much to be learned; some old preconceptions, notions and traditions must be abolished and new and vigorous concepts developed.

PART ONE

DEER IN THEIR ENVIRONMENT

CHAPTER I

DEER IN BRITAIN—HISTORY, HABITAT, HABITS

The deep and growing interest in deer today, especially in their conservation and betterment, can only be the result of a long-standing involvement with them. There can be no doubt but that their existence is known to date from prehistoric days, for there is evidence, through excavations and archaeological findings, that at least two of the remaining deer species have inhabited the British Isles since the Pleistocene. In his book *British Deer and Their Horns* (1897) J. G. Millais accounts for eleven early varieties of deer, including *Cervus elaphus* (red deer) and *Cervus capreolus* (roe deer). Fallow deer (*Dama dama*) do not appear in these prehistoric findings, the theory being that they may have been brought to Britain very much later by the Romans. But some scientists maintain that fallow deer moved out of Britain as the icecap advanced and never returned of their own volition, whereas red and roe deer either did return, or survived the ice age by adaptation.

These archaeological findings suggest that both red and roe deer of prehistoric days carried antlers of a shape identical—or at least similar—to their present-day successors, although some antlers of early red deer have been considerably larger. This theory is given proof in the illustrations to Millais's work, three of which are reproduced here (p 65), showing a reconstructed red deer head, of some 5ft span, one of normal size, and a selection of roe deer heads which, being of some 11in in length, are only marginally in excess of the present average.

In spite of the fact that there are no consecutive progressions of archaeological records to furnish really complete data concerning the species, historical records bear witness to the fact that deer have formed part of man's environment ever since the pre-Christian era. Tribal warfare and tribal hunger accounted for the early development of weapons—both those to be used against man and those to be used against beasts—and, as sophistication increased in man, so did he improve his instruments of death. The original clubs and slings were replaced by the earliest bows and arrows; vegetable creepers—used as nets or snares—gave way to traps in the form of balanced boulders, suspended spears and poisoned darts; then came the crossbow. Firearms, of course, were not used in the pursuit of deer until much later. (In Sutherland they were unknown until about the end of the sixteenth century, when a sort of blunderbuss, called a *glasnabhean*, was first introduced: but the conventional bow and arrow did not completely disappear until the middle of the seventeenth century.) From the pursuit of game on foot developed the pursuit of game on horseback, and the quarry had changed from being primarily the source of meat to being the source of pleasure, although the ritual of the chase long outlived its strictly functional necessity.

Not all, however, were allowed to indulge in this new form of recreation, and there must have been many who, perforce connected with it, did not find it as recreational as it might have been; as Pascal was to point out, a gentleman sincerely believed that hunting was a great and royal sport, but a beater was not of that opinion. The chase of the deer was restricted, as early as the time of King Canute, to the whim of royalty and the aristocracy, and the game laws of 1016 in Britain protected the king's beasts, and the king's forests, on pain of death, whilst the right to hunt beyond the royal lands was strictly limited to ownership. This prerogative extended through Norman times when, although new laws and habits were introduced, the forest laws remained much the same as formerly.

One detail of interest emerges from the Saxon period—the introduction of hunting calls to Britain, used in this country and on the Continent to this day for fox-hunting and deer-hunting.

There is a possibility, however, that hunting horns were used, on the Continent at least, at a very much earlier date, for the Solutré (Lyons) discoveries of whistle-like pipes, made of deer horn and conceivably used to give signals during the chase, can be dated to about 40,000 BC and are the precursors of the *corne de chasse* and the smaller English hunting horn.

From the twelfth and thirteenth centuries onwards, deer make their appearance in literature and fable as well as law—not only as the sport of kings but also as the more surreptitious quarry of Everyman. The first indication of 'poacher turned gamekeeper' can be found in Chaucer's 'Doctor's Tale', where it is suggested that

> A thief of venison, that hath forlaft
> His likerousness and all his olde craft
> Can kepe a forest best of any man

and the convert could then presumably exercise his new-found righteousness in the many enclosures and deer parks that sprang up to protect the nobility's beasts. In Tudor times, every manor house of the slightest pretension had a deer park, sometimes two— one for fallow and one for red deer. 'On hunting mornings the chime of hounds, "matched in mouth like bells" chased the deer round and round the enclosure, while the gentlemen and ladies of the manor and their guests followed easily on horseback' (Trevelyan, *English Social History*).

But deer still roamed wild over the Pennines, the Cheviots and the southern and northern moors, often hunted 'par-force' in an older tradition—for historical records show that during the reign of Elizabeth a pack of stag-hounds was kennelled at Simonsbath for this purpose. The method of stalking was not introduced as a 'gentleman's' way of hunting deer until many years later. In the south, fallow deer ran wild in the forests and the fens, often raiding the crops—and thus enclosures were built not only to keep the deer in but also now to keep the deer out.

Deer were hunted as sport, but they also formed a substantial part of the English diet of the time. Just as fishponds were constructed to furnish the table on Fridays and fast-days, so deer were kept to provide meat for the household. Fynes Moryson, writing shortly after the death of Elizabeth I, notes that

> The English have an abundance of white meats, of all kinds of flesh, fowl and fish of all things good for food. In the seasons of the year the English eat fallow deer plentifully, as bucks in the summer and does in winter which they bake in pastries, and this venison is a dainty, rarely found in any other kingdom. England, yea, perhaps one County thereof, hath more fallow deer than all Europe I have seen.

The Norman statutes not only remained as law but were even more strictly enforced, for in 1671 the Cavalier Parliament excluded freeholders of under £100 per annum from the right of killing game even on their own land. From then on, the sport declined, increasingly confined to the pleasure of those who could afford to keep land for this privilege, whilst others gave way to the increasing demand for agriculture and the beginnings of industry in England. In the north of England and particularly in Scotland, however, deer still held their place as widely recognised sport and, in the eighteenth and nineteenth centuries—to judge by the evidence which Millais used for his illustrations—heads were recorded whose excellence is nowadays, for a variety of reasons, seldom matched. The quarry of the kings became, in its turn, the monarch of the glens.

The British deer of today is, therefore, a creature of long history and parentage. Its position has changed somewhat in the last hundred years, from being the abundant property of a privileged few to being the less plentiful quarry of a much broader cross-section of sportsmen generally and, as such, the object of a much more general interest. With this general interest comes, one hopes, a more general understanding, knowledge and concern not only for sport but for heritage; for if the original and necessary reasons for killing beasts have vanished, the ritual and the habit have remained and, in the natural way of such things, men have learned to give respect to that from which they have derived pleasure. There is also the added question of a belated attempt at preserving that heritage, and of ensuring that the decline into which British deer have fallen is not, of necessity, permanent—for, in his attempts at civilisation and progress, man, in his usual paradoxical fashion, inevitably destroys that which he will most regret.

Andrew Sinclair, in *The Last of the Best*, remarks that 'It is odd that a passion for bloodsports should lead to such a responsibility for conservation.' Yet it has been proved, from Chaucer onwards (and is still being proved with increasing emphasis), that, as man's capabilities develop and his power and knowledge increase, his dearest wish is to recapture and preserve that Garden of Eden which he has laid waste by his own progress; and just as it is only by his own efforts that he has achieved that destruction, so only by his own efforts can he hope to attempt to create its artificial counterpart.

BASIC HABITAT REQUIREMENTS

By nature all deer are forest- and bush-dwellers. Whilst they will live in almost any woodland, they thrive best in deciduous forests, especially those containing beech, oak, birch and larch; chestnut of both horse and spanish variety are their favourites. It is not often that woodland is found without water; and although they do need water in their natural surroundings, deer, especially roe, will take enough water in the form of dew with their early morning feed to manage without access to water for some time.

Roe deer particularly, but also fallow deer, need thick cover where they can lie up during the day and chew, sun themselves in small open clearings and sleep. When living near agricultural areas, this is why they will live in the fields of corn, until harvest time, finding plenty of good food and adequate cover. Red deer when living in a forest will normally find thick cover too, but they can survive without it, and indeed, in Scotland, often do not bother to seek cover even if it is available.

Cover is important to all deer's wellbeing and maintenance of condition, on two counts. On hot summer days it provides shade, in which animals may get away from flies. Stags and fallow buck suffer a great deal from flies while their antlers are developing and are covered by living tissue known as velvet, particularly during the period when the velvet dries off, when the flies are attracted by the smell of drying blood and tissue. In consequence during that time they will seek escape in the form of thicket and shade, or else on high hilltops, which, being cooler and windier, are less fly-infested than the lower land. In the winter the deer's need for cover is even greater; firstly on account of food, which is often easier to come by, if only in the form of bark; secondly, more important, as a shelter from the weather. Deer are particularly sensitive to cold, and there are records of some found suffering from frostbite, especially that of the antlers in roe deer.

It has to be remembered that all species of deer go through winter under the most adverse conditions. Neither stags nor fallow buck fully recover from the rut before winter comes, and thus in a weakened state they have to face the adversities of bad weather. Their females are in the early months of pregnancy and require as much food and warmth as they can find. The roe buck develops his antlers throughout winter and is therefore particularly prone to frostbite; his female is luckier in that she has the benefit of dormant gestation which sees her through at least a part of the cold season.

Wherever they live, however, deer adapt themselves quickly to the habitat and, equally, react to changes of habitat. Thus, moved to more favourable conditions, they quickly develop better antlers and bigger bodies, provided they are accepted by the local deer, and such acceptance cannot always be guaranteed; cases have been recorded of imported deer being molested by the indigenous ones to a point of migration and even extinction—it is particularly the stags and bucks that react strongly to the intrusion of newcomers.

Another example of adaptation to environment is the partial change in eating habits. For instance, it is authoritatively stated in some parts of the world that deer will not eat ferns: yet in Scotland they do—especially during the months of July and August when the ferns are young and green. Also in the Cairngorms grassland is apparently less used by deer in summer—in contrast, for instance, with Rhum.

Equally, their reaction to change can be dramatic; for instance, who would credit the fact that, taken off the Scottish hills and fed under experimental conditions, a stag's first head can be an eight to ten pointer and its body can weigh some eleven stone at the age of ten to eleven months? Yet this has happened. One might say that it is not what we are after, because good deer management is not the same as 'deer farming'. However, 'deer farming', especially for experimental purposes, does mean that one can establish the potential of deer development under optimal conditions and then make the appropriate allowances for wild deer in their natural surroundings.

Less dramatic, but perhaps more acceptable results have been obtained where hill deer management has been placed on a 'proper' footing including a carefully worked out selective shooting plan and by partial feeding during the winter, either by bringing food to the deer or allowing deer access to food on lower agricultural or pasture areas, after harvesting has been completed; or, in recognition of the animals' seasonal needs, planting food in deer areas and allowing deer access to such planting during winter months, or even improving natural pasture by dressing or other means.

There are some who deprecate this winter feeding because it is artificial, saying that deer, being wild, have no business to be thus aided artificially; yet, surely the deer's environment is in itself artificial? It is free from predators, and the deer are subject to containment in living space, sometimes controlled in numbers, and not necessarily in healthy condition. Having upset the balance of nature we have to restore it, and one of the means of restoration is to cull selectively and feed judiciously.

If we follow these basic aims, deer will not only be restored to prime condition but will be able to play an important part in the national economy.

PARK DEER

A great deal of our knowledge of deer comes from observation of deer in park conditions. Indeed, a proportion of the 'wild' deer population of Britain is originally of park stock having escaped and avoided recapture. Certainly of the many varieties of deer in the British Isles today only the roe can claim that the chance of having park ancestry is remote; red deer in many areas, especially outside Scotland, are of park stock, and certainly fallow have park ancestry. The others, like Japanese sika and muntjack, now well-established in the British countryside, are relatively new 'escapees' from the parks.

The well-established deer park proves to us what can be done to maintain a high-value herd by means of careful feeding and culling. It could be argued that this is relatively simple under park conditions, but not so easy in the wild. There can be only one answer: it may not be easy, but at the same time it is not impossible. To achieve comparable success under wild conditions, it is necessary to get to know one's deer and to know their potential and limitations and also the potential of the environment.

DEER PSYCHOLOGY

Deer psychology is an important consideration, and one which suggests a variety of approaches to the problem of deer management. There are wide differences between the species, particularly so between red deer and roe deer and these are examined below. Fallow deer's characteristics differ from place to place, being more controlled by the environment in which they live and less 'stable' than the other two species.

RED DEER

Red deer live in herds which, basically, are segregated by sex for most of the year; the size of herd varies depending on the density of deer population.

The hind herd contains hinds with their young, those of both the current year and the preceding year. Additionally, the hind herd normally includes immature stags, the older of these probably just approaching the age of puberty.

Under normal conditions, the herd leader is a healthy middle-aged hind, rarely below the age of eight years, usually with a calf. Her leadership is the main and most important influence over the behaviour of the entire herd which will rely on her senses and 'judgement'; for the leading hind usually has the most highly developed instinct, probably resulting from her role as a mother. She will usually be at the forefront of the herd whilst on the move; she selects the feeding area, leads the herd to cover or away from danger and selects suitable resting places. Hence the constitution of the herd on the move is as follows: first, the leading hind a few yards ahead of her current year's calf, with the previous year's calf following; these three are followed by other hinds, each with a calf, and by those hinds which have recently lost their young. Then come the old, calfless hinds, then the young stags in order of age, the younger preceding the older. This sequence is retained while the herd is undisturbed on the move and will be broken only in a moment of panic.

It is the responsibility of the leading hind to ascertain that the passage is safe; she takes that responsibility very seriously and the rest follow her directives instinctively. It is for this reason that the leading hind continually maintains a look-out, and the herd join her only when she has ensured their safety. This leader-to-herd relationship is particularly evident in woodland, where the leading hind can be seen standing at the edge of the cover, surveying the more open area, before moving out to be followed by the rest.

Once the feeding area is reached, the leading hind will deploy the look-outs, whilst she feeds, and she will periodically 'inspect' the look-outs herself.

It must be evident by now that the role of the leading hind is a vital one, and if she is eliminated the entire herd system is upset, if not completely disorganised. In a situation where the leading hind is shot, the remainder, being deprived of the leader, are in confusion. Instances are known where the entire herd has refused to move any distance, stopping, turning and returning to the original spot. Often in this situation the herd splits—new leaders being established by selection or usurping leadership before the order returns. It is important that, when hind groupings are small, the leading hind should never be shot. Conversely, if hind herds are larger than desired, the shooting of the leading hind may result in the required split-up of the herd.

Frequently a herd of hinds is intolerant and will act on the basis of the survival of the fittest, refusing to accept the sick, weak and ailing and rejecting these animals from the herd. The rejects, for a time, remain close to the herd but ultimately divorce themselves from it; thus the single hinds or single young must be suspect and are of high priority in the shooting plan.

Until the rutting season, the constitution of the herd is as described above, and at the opening of the rut the stags—perhaps other than the one- and maybe two-year-olds—leave the herd, whilst the youngsters are usually chased out by the old stag taking charge of the herd. At the conclusion of the rut the young stags return to the hind herd, but the older group which was hitherto with the hinds may well join the stags rather than the hinds, having by now reached the age of sex maturity.

Whilst the herds of hinds are mixed in relation to their ages, stags form their herds differently. Herds of stags rarely exceed twenty, although in a high density situation larger numbers are possible. In winter, the herds divide into smaller groupings, possibly because of greater feeding problems. The larger groupings of stags normally consist of younger animals, those up to the age of six to eight years, whilst the older ones form their own smaller groups, admitting the younger sometimes as look-outs. The old stags, usually those above the age of ten, tend to live in groups as small as two or three, probably allowing one middle-aged companion; these are the most timid groups, seeking cover during daylight, or lying up well concealed in broken ground yet having a good spying position.

The leadership instinct is not as clearly marked in stags as it is in hinds; all one can say is that in older groups the middle-aged often leads, preceding the older companions. It is not known for certain how the stag becomes 'elected', but it would be reasonable to assume that the middle-aged animal has more acute awareness than his older companions, with a modicum of initiative and common sense.

During the period of antler growth, the herds of stags keep to the high or well-covered ground, trying to avoid fly-infested areas. Once their antlers are fully developed and clear of velvet, the stags disband into small groups until, by the opening of the rut, it is rare to see stags in groups of more than two or three unless they are young. As the older ones come to the end of their rutting so the younger groups fall apart, each animal attempting to win mastery of a herd of hinds. After the post-rutting rest, the stags start congregating again, to remain in their all-male groups until the next year's rut.

The pattern of behaviour of red deer is such that it can adjust to the environment. Whether in wooded or open land, it undergoes only small changes. For instance, it is not uncommon to see a hind, with only her ears and eyes protruding over a rock or bluff, or her face round a boulder, surveying the hill before she emerges, just as her woodland sister would use a bush. It is common to see the stag lying down in a good spying position, covering the approaches to him; similarly he would survey a forest glade from a position of advantage. Their senses soon get accustomed to distance, to wind eddies and to turns of the open hillside.

ROE DEER

One of the reasons why the roe has to adapt its habits more radically to life in the open (if indeed it will adapt at all) is that it relies more on smell and hearing, and less on eyesight, than the red deer. In comparison, its eyesight is poor. Consequently its use of open land is limited, especially in the summer, when strong thermal convections carry smell upwards. Thus roe relies more on its extremely acute hearing in the first place and reacts immediately to any suspicious or unfamiliar sound. A roe is therefore sometimes less disturbed by a loud undisguised sound than by an obviously muffled or concealed one. It is suggested that one of the reasons why 'field roe' lives in groupings is that the group's 'joint' ability to detect danger is greater than that of the individual.

The timid behavioural pattern of roe needs some study. To see and hear clearly the roe has to have its head up: if satisfied of its safety, it will continue feeding but, once disturbed or suspicious, it will suddenly lift its head and watch, listen and smell. This pattern is more marked in the open than in areas of good cover where, if in danger, the roe will move for denser cover, completely noiselessly, provided it knows that it has not been spotted, barking in flight usually only when surprised or startled.

Whilst roe do not normally live in herds and keep mainly to small family groups of a doe and a fawn—possibly with the inclusion of the previous year's young and another doe—they resort nevertheless to small communities, especially during winter. At the beginning of spring groups divide; does with young separate from the groups, some returning to the previous year's territory and others seeking new areas. Basically, however, does do not develop the feeling of territorial possessiveness.

On the other hand, roe buck are very possessive of their territory. Even in early spring the buck will mark his domain and fight for it, for it is his feeding and living area, over which he allows no interference. The denser the roe population, the more he guards his 'frontiers'. His territorial requirements vary from ten to forty acres, but he will eagerly establish himself in a greater area if he can. The tougher the buck, the more likely he is to take a choice location from the point of view of feeding and safety, expelling the younger and weaker. It is during the period of marking his territory that the buck will bark, scrape the ground with his forelegs, fray young trees and bushes and urinate along his 'march'. If or when the 'place buck' is killed or dies, younger buck will move in and fight for the area as an entirety, or for parts of it, each attempting to mark his own domain, hence the killing of an old 'place buck' often leads to some damage being done by the newcomers.

There is among the buck a strong social hierarchy, the top of the structure being taken by the prime buck of the area; all the younger, weaker buck have to subordinate themselves. This hierarchical system is clearly marked at the opening of the rut, when the prime buck claims his does; fights develop when two buck consider themselves to have equal rights to primacy.

The buck's territorial and hierarchical ambitions vanish during the period in which he grows new antlers and is sexually inactive. He will, however, re-establish himself at the end of spring, and will lead an anti-social life until the rut. During the rut he will follow a doe and will stay with her for a time, until she moves out of his area to mate with another buck. Following a period of rest after the rut he may tend to rejoin the does, rarely more than two, and stay with them over winter.

THE REPRODUCTIVE CYCLE

If we are to manage and control deer, we must attempt to understand their reproductive cycle as that which most closely affects their behavioural pattern.

THE MALE

Apart from sex organs themselves, there are related secondary characteristics, the most important of which are the antlers; except in reindeer, these are the male deer's prerogative.

Antlers are regrown annually except for the 'first head' which takes up to fifteen months before it is clear of velvet. From year to year as the animal develops in maturity the antlers grow bigger in size and weight, and the number of tines increases, normally until the prime is reached; the antlers retain the general characteristics of shape and form from year to year (Fig 1 and p 66), unless damage of substantial nature is sustained either to the body or to the pedicle. (Certain types of damage, disease or wounds to the body, particularly to the sex organs, legs, liver, lungs and kidney, and bone breaks of the antler pedicle often result in lasting and recurring malformations of antler. These are described in *Wild Deer* by the author.) Prime antler is grown or regrown for one to three years with only minor yearly changes, but after that time the antler tends to deteriorate from year to year, 'going back' in size and number of tines, but not necessarily in the thickness of

1 Antler characteristics. The main characteristics of the antler, as denoted in the basic shape, are retained from year to year, in spite of the change of number of tines (see also photo on page 66).

the beam. The size and condition of the prime antler, as well as the age at which it is reached, depend largely on the living conditions of the animals and their state of health. Furthermore, there is a strong aspect of heredity; characteristics are passed by both parents to their young—thus the stag's characteristics may be passed through his female offspring to her young male. These characteristics of the antler can therefore be retained, subject to suitable living conditions; hence, under certain circumstances one can maintain or develop a type of antler such as 'Warnham', or 'Endsleigh', or 'Lakeland', or indeed 'Scottish type'.

At times which differ between the species, and are age-related, antlers are shed annually and regrown annually. The antler develops and grows under the cover of a soft furry skin (velvet), under which there is a living tissue of horn through which the blood flows. At the end of the annual growth cycle the antler virtually dies and hardens; the blood flow stops, the velvet dries and is rubbed away.

The yearly antler development is controlled by the annual sex cycle as related to the annual development of testes as Fig 2 indicates.

An investigation into the effects of castration of the Virginian deer (see Ref 1) showed that the antler cycle in the species is regulated by both the testes and the pituitary gland. The pituitary gland is responsible for stimulating the growth of new antlers; the hormone produced by the testes is necessary both for the hardening of the antlers and for the shedding of velvet which occurs when the testes are increasing in activity. The antlers are shed after the rut, when the activity of the testes declines; an injection of testicular hormone, just before the antlers are due to be shed, results in their being retained for longer than is the case with normal deer (Ref 2).

Most deer's antler development cycles are 'staggered', the yearling cleaning the velvet off his antlers last whilst the older animals clean theirs first. Conversely, the older animals shed their antlers before the younger ones. These characteristics, being the result of the cycle of activity of the testes, indicate visibly that the older stag or buck enters the rut before the younger one. However, the shedding can also be influenced to a degree by the fluctuations of weather in the locality. The growth and shedding cycles also differ between the locations, probably as a result of varying climatic and feeding conditions. These differences can be a matter of days, even weeks; for instance, the cycle in North Germany takes place some 3–4 weeks earlier than in Scotland, which in turn is two weeks later than in the West Country or Thetford Chase.

The age at which a male is first able to fertilise a female differs between species and between individual animals; furthermore the park deer may differ from the wild animals. Basically, Scottish red deer show their sexual maturity in the third year but they do not always rut in that year, and even if they do, they may be prevented from fertilising a female by the older stags. A fallow buck reaches puberty probably in the second or third year and a roe during his third year, even though younger bucks, those in the second year, have been known to chase the doe at the end of the rut.

RUTTING

The characteristics and behavioural pattern of rutting varies substantially between species.

Red deer The red deer stag collects a group of hinds which he defends from all challengers, marking his territory by means of secretions from the lachrymal and metatarsal glands, by urinating and, in the woodland, by threshing trees and bushes. He announces his presence by a typical roar. Having established his territory and his harem, the size of which differs from year to year (the variables being the number of hinds available and the competition from other stags —in other words, animal density and sex ratio), his rutting period, depending on his age, will fall somewhere between mid-September and the end of October and could last into November, depending on the weather and climatic conditions of the location.

36

Fallow deer The fallow buck does not collect a harem, but the female moves into the buck's rutting area and moves from one area to another (and therefore from one buck to another); thus the buck defends his rutting place rather than his females. The marking of the rutting location is done in a similar fashion to red deer. The fallow buck develops a rutting 'groan' or 'grunt', rather that the roar of the red deer stag; this grunt is lost at the end of the rut. The normal time for fallow rut is about October–November with some advance or delay caused by weather.

Roe deer The behavioural pattern of roe during the rut is quite different from the other two species. The rut takes place much earlier in the year, normally between June and August, depending on location; the further north, the later it is, and it lasts about two weeks. The buck defends his territory in the same way as the fallow buck and spends most of his courtship within it. The roe

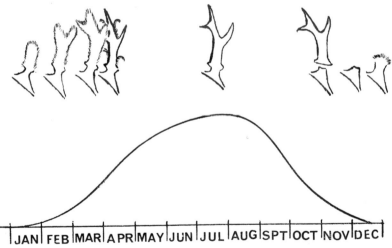

| JAN | FEB | MAR | A PR | MAY | JUN | JUL | AUG | SPT | OCT | NOV | DEC |

2 Antler and sex development in the yearly cycle. There is a direct relationship between the size of testes and the hormonal activity (depicted by the curve) and the annual development of antlers. Whilst this figure presents the roe buck's cycle, a similar cycle can be drawn up for red and fallow deer but, of course, to a different timing (approximately four months later).

have been thought to be monogamous because the buck pursues only one female at a time, but the does move from one buck to another. In courtship, the buck chases the doe in circles, referred to as 'roe rings', or sometimes in a figure of eight, two rings, a left-handed and a right-handed, being immediately together. The centre of the ring is often a bush or a small tree; the rings are frequently used by a buck for several years running. The rutting is not completely confined, however, to the June–August period; a second rut does occur with a smaller number of animals in October or November; this is of more frequent occurrence than is usually appreciated.

All three species The activities of the rutting period do cause a considerable deterioration of the male deer's general condition. They lose a great deal of weight and become much less resistant to disease. As far as deer management is concerned, therefore, there is a problem particularly regarding red and fallow deer. These deer start the winter in a poorer state of health than they held at the end of the summer; this is an important consideration which must be borne in mind when thinking of the animals' access to food. In addition to the problem of general health and weight, this is the period when the roe deer antler goes through intensive growth, again requiring adequate and suitable nourishment.

Fortunately, immediately after the rut, the males and females separate, and both, after a period of rest, feed intensively to recover their condition.

THE FEMALE

The period of heat (the oestrus) is normally confined to the period of rut when the female comes into season. Red and fallow deer have been thought to have only one period of heat in a year, but instances have been recorded of red deer hind coming into season late in the year, even in winter, being covered by a stag, and producing the young later than is usual. Similar occurrences in roe have been recorded as late as January.

Under normal wild conditions, the oestrus probably first occurs in the third year of a hind's life, although there are indications that a three-year-old hind can already have had a calf, thus having been fertilised in the second year. Fallow does are also thought to come on heat for the first time in their third year, but there are exceptions. The roe doe would appear to come on heat at about the age of two.

Having been fertilised, the female's gestation period is about 220–250 days. Here we have a basic difference between the roe and other species: roe have a period of dormant gestation and consequently, in instances of late implantation, are still capable of producing young at the normal time, which is about the end of May after about 140 days of development. On the other hand, the late implantation of red or fallow deer results in a late birth. For this reason there is a strong school of thought that in a case of late rut of red or fallow deer, the hind and the stag (or doe and buck) should be shot; the male, because he becomes very weakened by the rutting in winter, and the female because she will produce a weak and late offspring.

In broad terms, therefore, the dropping season for red deer and fallow is about June. Roe deer drop their fawns in late May or early June, but variations in these times cover a fairly wide span.

Whilst examining the breeding cycle of deer, one should remember that the female, whether covered or not, is not producing a calf every year but has a 'rest' every now and again. How often these 'rests' occur is difficult to say, and the studies so far are not fully reliable. The estimates range from no rest at all, in respect of some animals, to one every three years in others. The importance of this factor is that, when shooting hinds, those females without a calf should not automatically be shot; it is fairly certain that after a 'rest' the hind or doe produces a very strong youngster.

THE CALF AND FAWN

Much has been said about the numbers of calves or fawns that are born. The facts are that, whilst with red deer and fallow deer twins are uncommon, with roe they are not unusual, and even triplets have been recorded. Where twins are born, there is no established proof that either they are or are not both of the same sex.

The young become agile within hours of birth and remain with their mother for a fair period of time, suckling her in spite of the fact that they are capable of taking solid food from very early. Red and fallow deer lactate as late as January and February.

The mortality among fawns and calves is an important consideration. Pre-natal mortality would appear to be low; the post-natal mortality depends on the density of predators who take a large proportion of young deer, but with a normal density of foxes and eagles, and allowing for disease mortality, which can be high, a survival of 50 per cent must be expected and, at a low limit of mortality, 75 per cent is likely.

CHAPTER 2

BODY AND TOOTH DEVELOPMENT AS AIDS TO RECOGNITION

Over the past years of growing interest in deer management, within the deer owning and stalking circles deer recognition has taken a prominent place in literature, research, training and even competitions and exhibitions.

The reason for this is clear. The better the recognition and classification of the beasts, the more effective the management of deer is going to be. To this end, therefore, two main avenues of recognition need exploring and improving: first, the ability to classify live beasts on the hoof quickly—especially when stalking—and effectively and therefore accurately when both stalking and managing deer; second, the ability to establish accurately the class and age of deer either killed or found dead, in order to be able to assess the fine adjustment which the stock may require to conform to the predetermined age structure. One cannot equate the two skills, for the need for almost subconscious, instantaneous reaction and decision necessary in the stalking situation is different from the leisurely procedure which can be adopted when ageing a dead beast.

The need for accurate recognition having been established, the stalker must call on nature and human ingenuity to help him, and on a variety of science-based but practical and quick methods of age classification which have been developed. Provided all newly born calves can be caught and marked, such aids and methods as coloured tags attached to the ear, collars round the neck, or shaped small nicks in the ears can be used. Under wild conditions, however, these aids are not always possible, and in any case many would oppose them on principle as gimmicky, uneconomic, etc. The most common method, therefore, is the stalker's skill in recognition of the animal itself, on the hill or in woodland, mainly by the shape and size of its body and, in the case of the male, by the antlers. Indeed, a first-class local professional stalker ought to know his deer well enough to be able to recognise each male 'personally' year after year, and many do. This intimate knowledge and quick recognition of the beasts provides the most infallible method of deciding the shootability of any given deer. If a stalker can affirm to himself that he has known a particular beast for let us say twelve years, and that the last two heads have been deteriorating, he then has the confidence to decide whether to shoot or not to shoot.

There are a variety of characteristics which guide the stalker in determining the shootability of a beast, and the important ones are the antler and body build; chapter 3 is devoted to the analysis of antler characteristics; here we concentrate upon the body, and tooth formation.

BODY BUILD

A deer below the age of one year is the familiar Disney Bambi, with long ears, long legs, a small head, short body and large, black, pleading eyes which look inquisitively at everything. Its gait knows no half measures; it either places each leg carefully and slowly taking high steps, or leaps and bounds, the latter with considerable stamina, when some four to six months old.

As the bones develop and the flesh-cover thickens, the head enlarges to normal size, and the ears lose their appearance; the

3 (*Facing page*) Red deer recognition by body shape. Note the elevation of the young stag's head. Note the ears of the old animals which tend to 'turn back', also deep thick neck of the old stag when compared with the young; slope in the rump is another useful indication of age. The old mature hind leads with her young calf following; the weak hind could be the previous year's calf (therefore not fully mature), or an older beast which has not grown well. Note the old hind's long neck and muzzle.

3 years   Yearling   4-6 years

7-8 years

Very old   Old

Old hind   Calf   Weak hind

43

Old buck - 9 years or older

Medium aged (4-6 years)

Young buck (2-3 years)

4 (*Facing page and above*) Roe deer recognition by body build. Note the difference in the thickness of the body generally and the neck particularly. The elevation of the head of an undisturbed animal is an infallible sign of age.

neck starts filling and the whole body grows longer and deeper.

A three-year-old red or fallow deer is almost full-size; although the animal is fully mature, the appearance is still young, mainly on account of the head being long and held high and erect, the neck extending upwards from the almost straight-backed body and with the antlers still a long way from being fully developed. The first signs of the mane appear at about this age.

With advancing age the disproportionate length of the face vanishes as it fills outwards; the hitherto pointed muzzle becomes more stubby, and the neck fills and becomes deeper, especially as the mane grows longer.

The shoulders, which in the first four years seem to fall into a straight line of the back, start forming a small hump at the base of the neck protruding upwards until, at the age of about nine to ten, the line breaks above the shoulder, falling downwards towards the base of the neck and towards the rump. This elevation of the shoulder points becomes more pronounced as from the eighth year onwards the head is carried lower. A very old stag carries his head so low that he appears to be looking downwards, with the frontal bone of the head almost at right angles to the ground and the antlers almost vertically 'balanced' upon the head (Fig 3).

The roe loses its Bambi appearance at the age of nine to twelve months. In the second year as the body fills out only the face remains youthful, perhaps on account of the still smallish head and the large ears almost overshadowing the antlers.

A well-developed and healthy roe of three years (second head) should have changed its winter coat to summer colour by end of May to mid-June whilst the older animals may still be changing theirs. At this age the animal is fully developed in the body, and the indication of age is obtained from the manner in which the animal holds its head—high and erect.

At four years the neck fills out and the antlers are then more or less full-size, even if still on the thin side. From this age onwards the neck fills out quickly and the head is carried lower and lower from year to year, until, as is the case with red deer, an old buck gives an impression of looking downwards when he is eight or nine years old (Fig 4).

Whilst it may not be too difficult to assess the age of the male deer because much guidance is gained from the formation of the antlers, the female represents more of a problem. The notes that follow describe characteristics of red deer hinds. These characteristics can also be applied to fallow deer does and, provided allowance is made for age, to roe deer does. As a general yardstick, one could halve the age of hind and arrive at the characteristics of a roe doe.

The hinds can be divided into four groups:

1 Female calves and very young hinds below the age of fertility (roe does up to the age of 18–20 months)
2 Young but fertile hinds aged 3–5 years (roe does 2–3 years)

3 Fully mature hinds at the peak of reproductive ability, aged 6–10 years (roe deer does 3–6 years)
4 Old hinds and old does

(1) Female calves and very young hinds (does). A young hind up to the age of about 2 years is smaller in the shoulder than the older animals; in a herd it will normally follow behind the most recent calf following the mother (who is usually the mother, or adopted mother, of both). A fairly good indicator of a yearling and a young hind is the length of the head which assumes full length by the age of 2½ years. At 2½ years the animal is about fully developed; the hitherto noticeable slimness of the body disappears.

(2) From 3 to 5 years the hind's head and body start filling in until—

(3) By the time she reaches 5 the hind's body looks sturdy and well filled; a well-developed animal should not show her ribs, other than perhaps at the end of winter. A useful point to watch is the ears. Until the animal is of advanced age, say about 9, the ears change direction quickly, appearing firm and fully responsive to the reflexes which make them move.

(4) Over the age of 10, the neck of a hind starts to get thinner, the lower neck starts to develop a mane-like long growth, the shoulder and the withers become more pronounced and the ribs may well be visible through the skin for most of the year. With advancing age the entire head appears longer and more emaciated; the ears become flabby and even droop somewhat, especially in the sideways or forward configuration; they certainly have a marked up-and-down flapping movement when the hind moves along. The old hind without a calf is normally at the end of the herd, just before the young stags, and very rarely retains her leadership of the herd after the age of 10 or 11. Old hinds' calves are often weaker than their contemporaries of younger mothers, because the old beasts tend to be impatient, and poor mothers; hence old hinds or does with young can be shot without much risk.

From the point of view of selection in culling, needless to say the old hinds and does, specially those noted to have weak young, and those out of condition or obviously diseased, must be taken. It is difficult to summarise the outward appearance of sickness but a few indications can be provided.

A clear indication of poor condition is the coat, which when the animal is in poor health will lose its lustre quite quickly; it subsequently becomes ruffled and ultimately even dirty. The animal tends to lose weight, and thus within a few days of the onset of disease or sickness, the ribs begin showing and the flanks cave in.

Red and fallow deer herds reject the diseased animals, which follow behind the herd, the space between them increasing as the speed of herd movement increases. Any attempt by a diseased animal to rejoin the herd is normally opposed by the rest, and several records exist of the herd fighting off the unwanted ill member. Fights among the hinds can be quite fierce; usually the attacking animal rears on its hind legs and hits out with its forelegs.

These phenomena of nature are not so noticeable in roe deer which do not live in herds; here, however, a single doe, without either a young or another female, is already suspect and the visible characteristics of ill-health are the same as those already described.

When confronted by a herd, it can be difficult to make a quick selection of which animal to shoot. Here again, certain points of guidance can be followed.

When a herd is on the move, it normally has an easily distinguishable leader. It has been observed that when the leader is shot the herd life is upset, and several potential leaders emerge. In consequence, if a herd larger than wanted is found, and needs to be split, the easiest and surest way is to shoot the leader. This is in fact the only occasion when the leader may be shot.

The centre of the herd is constituted of good-quality prime-aged females and their young, with older hinds closing the ranks, followed only by young stags.

From the above description come a few indicators:

1 The leading animal may not be shot, unless it is necessary to split the herd.

2 It is safer to shoot the animals from the rear part of the herd.

3 Lonely hinds are normally (calving season apart) the weaker or sick species and should be shot. Here, a word of warning: the leading animal often leaves the herd to 'spy out' the land, the herd remaining in cover. In this situation the leader is vulnerable and may be mistaken for a lonely beast; the leader is always in good physical condition.

The recognition of the female is a difficult problem which nevertheless has to be solved if selective shooting is to succeed. In deer species leading a gregarious life, much information can be gained by drawing a comparison between the appearance of the females and calves/fawns in the herd. The real problem is the roe which basically lives a single-family life and does not allow for a valid and sure comparison to be made. For this reason it may be

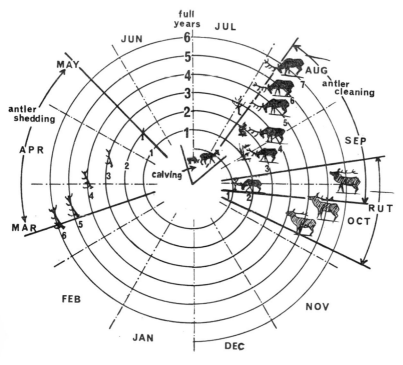

5   The Life Cycle of a Stag

advisable to add a few characteristics of a doe; whilst these characistics apply to other female deer, they are not quite as clear and noticeable as with the female roe deer.

In the first few months of life the female fawn is very difficult to distinguish from the male; the male is slightly bigger and has a blunter face than the female—these differences can be seen when the two are together, but the variation in size is minimal. The first marked difference between male and female comes with the development of antler pedicles; these are visible when the young is some four months old.

A young doe is light in body, and carries her head on a long, supple neck; her nature is 'skittish' and she tends to be inquisitive rather than timid; she uses her ears to exaggeration. These characteristics vanish when the young is about to produce her first offspring, when she becomes shy and very timid and suspicious. Her sleek body becomes 'well covered', the neck thickens and general behaviour becomes mature.

As she ages, from about 6 or 7, the neck and flanks start to become thinner, the face loses some of the flesh and therefore starts to appear longer, with vestiges of loose skin on the face. Her timidity increases and she is not often seen in the open, but rather seeks the safety of cover.

A characteristic of roe of both sexes is the grey patch above the nostrils, which grows and extends with age, giving the face a grey look with advancing years. Whilst it is not possible to establish the exact relationship between the age and this 'going grey', it is certain that a grey-looking face is that of an old animal.

In order to estimate the age of deer on the hoof other useful indications are in the relative time of coat changing, antler cleaning and shedding, and rutting, all of which differ between old and young. In all these characteristics, the older animals are 'ready' before the young; thus the antler shedding, velvet clearing and rut of the older take place before those of the younger. On the other hand, the coat changing is reversed; it is particularly noticeable in roe, where a young three-to-four-year-old buck should have its summer coat clean by the end of May whilst the older animals are

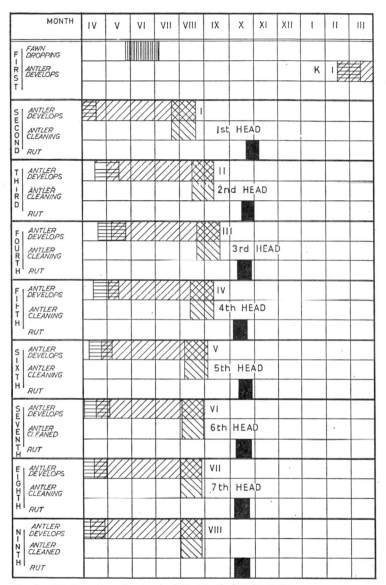

K – Possible formation of knobs   I = 1st head; II = 2nd head etc

Fawns dropped | Antler in velvet | Cleaning of velvet | Antler shedding | Rut

6   Antler Cycle of Fallow Deer

still changing theirs, especially in the neck and shoulder area, by mid-June. The time cycles of each of the species are shown in Figs 5, 6 and 7, but it has to be remembered that exact timing of the events is related to geographical and climatic conditions.

So far we have examined certain aspects of deer on the hoof which can give an indication as to whether the beast in question should be preserved or shot. Such knowledge as this is of great use, but cannot, and must not, be given more importance than that of practical and intimate knowledge of deer on an almost 'personal' level. This intimate knowledge is bound to be the prerogative of those who can, or should, be in daily contact with their deer throughout the year, such as the professional stalkers

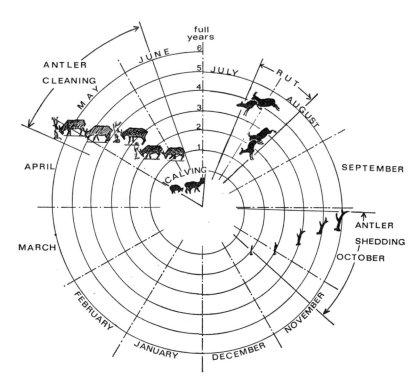

7   The Life Cycle of a Buck

and keepers, some of the resident owners and tenants, and also to a degree the shepherds and woodmen, who could and should help by providing valuable information about the animals. The prime responsibility, however, must rest with the keepers, who should know the deer on their land and be conversant with their habits and movements, reaction to weather, etc. Such knowledge can only be built up over time, through keen observation.

TOOTH FORMATION

Whilst recognition of the beasts by their outward appearance is an important factor in the execution of all shooting and management plans and is one without which many animals are bound to be shot mistakenly, the ability to judge accurately the age of animals either killed or found dead is an essential factor in planning and monitoring the cull. There are two reasons for this: first, one can build up over the years a precise age structure of the deer on the land, and second, one can decide what age groups should be included in the shooting plan for the next season, to ensure the proper age structuring of the animal stock on the ground. This more precise assessment of age can be made on the basis of tooth formation.

The basic principles upon which judging of age by tooth formation is applied are the same in all deer, but, because the life-span differs, the teeth of different species have to last for different lengths of time, and have different speeds of wear.

Table 1, Figs 8, 9 and 10 and p 83 give a variety of more or less standard approaches to age estimation by tooth formation. One has to remember that, over the years, numerous theories on age estimation have been developed, all of which prove that, other than by clinical means, completely accurate age estimation is virtually impossible, and even tooth wear must be accepted as only a fairly accurate indicator. The accuracy is to large degree a matter of practice and local knowledge; local knowledge, because it depends on the diet the deer find. The hardness of their teeth depends on the mineral content in their food and similar factors,

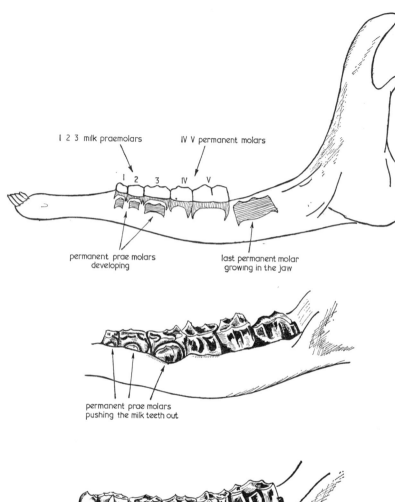

I 2 3 milk praemolars   IV V permanent molars

I 2 3 IV V

permanent prae molars
developing

last permanent molar
growing in the jaw

permanent prae molars
pushing the milk teeth out

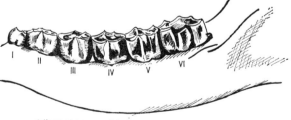

I II III IV V VI

full set of permanent teeth
(Roe deer at 13 months; Red deer at 30 months)

8   Basic development of teeth of the lower jaw, red and roe deer

TABLE I

LOWER JAW DEVELOPMENT

Age	Roe deer			Red deer		
	Incisors and canine	Praemolars*	Molars*	Incisors and canine	Praemolars*	Molars*
1 month	all milk	1, 2, 3	—	all milk	—	—
4 months	all milk	1, 2, 3	IV	all milk	1, 2, 3	—
6 months	all milk	1, 2, 3	IV, V			
8 months	1st perm	1, 2, 3	IV, V	all milk	1, 2, 3	IV
10 months	2nd perm	1, 2, 3	IV, V			
13 months	all perm	I, II, III	IV, V, VI	all milk	1, 2, 3	IV, V
1¼ years				1st perm	1, 2, 3	IV, V
1½ years				2nd perm	1, 2, 3	IV, V
2 years				all perm	1, 2, 3	IV, V
2½ years				all perm	I, II, III	IV, V, VI

* Arabic numerals denote milk teeth, roman numerals permanent teeth.

so that accuracy even within plus/minus two years may be impossible. Particular difficulties arise also in cases of malformation of the jaw, loss of some teeth, injuries, etc, for all of which some allowances have to be made.

A scientific, yet under careful conditions feasible, way of estimating age accurately is that developed by Eidman (Ref 3). His method relies upon the growth and regrowth of secondary dentine on the incisors, which reforms as the enamel wears down with age. If secondary dentine did not form, the tooth cavity would

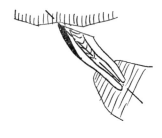

9 Age estimation by incisors. Note the angle of these teeth changing with age. (*top*) About 2 years; (*middle*) about 10 years; (*bottom*) about 14 years. Note also the lines formed by the secondary dentine formation. Seven layers in the middle tooth represent 10 years (Eidman method)

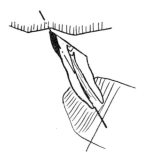

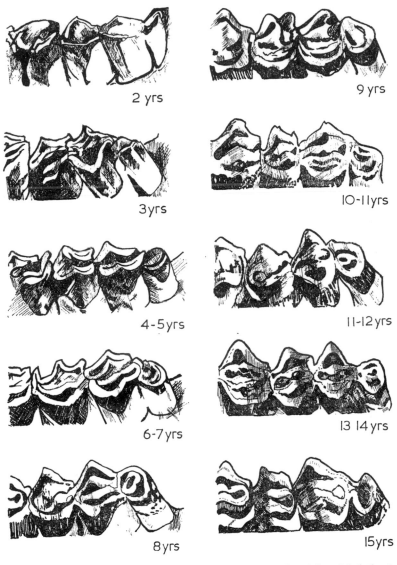

2 yrs

9 yrs

3yrs

10-11yrs

4-5yrs

11-12yrs

6-7yrs

13 14yrs

8yrs

15yrs

10 Age estimation by the wear of the third molar. The third (last) molar develops in red deer at the age of about 2½ years and roe deer at 12–13 months. It consists of three distinct sections, the last being the smallest. That section is subjected to steady and gradual wear, probably more steady than any other tooth (see also Table 2 for comparison between hard- and soft-tooth wear and the photographs on p 83 for illustration of wear)

be bared open, exposing the nerve to decay. To prevent this happening, layers of secondary dentine grow and, if the tooth is cut vertically in the fore-and-aft plane, the regrowth layers can be distinguished under a magnifying glass, each layer representing a year. This growth starts after three years of life, and so the number of layers plus three equals the animal's age. Eidman's method is accurate until a red deer is about ten years old, after which time the regrowth rate is slower. Another system, also developed by Eidman, is the wear of the crown and the angle of the incisors. The crown is worn down and at the same time there is a marked paradentoza (the roots of each tooth are slowly forced out of the jaw-bone). As a result, the angle of the incisors increases gradually

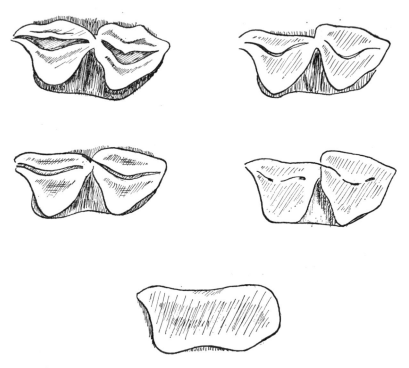

11 Shape of the register in the molar tooth. Referred to in Table 2 and graded as (*top left*) 'wide-open', (*centre left*) 'open', (*top right*) 'narrow', (*centre right*) 'disappearing' and (*below*) 'vanished'

from about 40° (from horizontal) at the age of three to more than 70° at the age of ten. An attempt to illustrate Eidman's method is in Fig 9.

Many experts place great emphasis on the wear of the third molar. This is the last tooth at the back of the bottom jaw, and it is of a treble build. The last section of it is high and narrow. This tooth is fully developed when the red deer is thirty months old (roe about eighteen months). From that age onwards, the high and narrow section is subject to gradual, regular and continuous wear, thus giving a good indication of age (Fig 11).

All these methods are valid, but all have to be used with some care; ideally every indication should be considered, and this is why, when attempting to estimate the age, one should use the entire jaw bone (both sides) and have access to the upper jaw, especially when unevenness is found.

Finally, an attempt to summarise the development of tooth formation and their gradual wear and to make allowance for tooth hardness, has been made in Table 2, which also differentiates between red and roe deer.

CHANGES IN TOOTH FORMATIO

2nd Praemolar Registers	3rd Praemolar Registers	1st molar Register	Dentine	2nd molar Register	Dentine	3rd molar Register	Dentine
		wide open	line	wide open	line		
Newly developed		open	narrow rhomb			Newly developed	
		narrow (closing)	rhomb				
wide open	very thin	open	narrow rhomb	open		wide open	line
open	thin	narrow (closing)	rhomb	narrow (closing)	rhomb	open	narrow rhomb
narrow (closing)	narrow	very narrow (nearly closed)	oval				
very narrow (nearly closed)	wide	dis-appearing	oval	very narrow (nearly closed)	oval	narrow	rhomb
disappearing	very wide	minimal (traces only)	whole area	dis-apppearing	oval	very narrow (nearly closed)	oval
traces only	whole area	vanished	whole area	traces only	whole area	dis-appearing	oval
vanished	whole area	teeth worn to roots		vanished	whole area	traces only	whole area
teeth worn to the roots, some falling out						vanished	whole area

ELATED TO AGE (ROE AND RED DEER)

	Roe			Red	
Yellow (soft dentine)	Brown	Black (hard dentine)	Yellow (soft dentine)	Brown	Black (hard dentine)
c	c	1	c	c	c
c	1		2½ years (30m)	2½ years (30m)	2½ years (30m)
1		2	3	4	4
	2	3			
2	3	3/4			
3	3/4	4/5	4	5	5/6
3/4	4/5	5/7	5	6/7	7/8
4/5	5/7	7/9	6/7	8	10
5/7	7/9	9/12	8/9	9/10	11/12
7/9	10+	11+	10	12	14
10+	12+	13+	12		16
			13/15	14	18

CHAPTER 3

CHARACTERISTICS OF ANTLER DEVELOPMENT

A great deal has been written concerning deer antlers, especially when good animals have been killed and the trophies become a matter of competition or local pride. But, all too often, those same splendid-looking antlers, whilst satisfying the desires of trophy-collectors, spell doom to the herd, which thereby lost a prime animal and often one capable of fathering generations of fine-quality offspring.

All too often beasts are killed because their antlers are considered to be rubbish, whilst even a superficial examination indicates that the 'rubbish' was never allowed to grow old enough to develop into a prime head.

MAIN CHARACTERISTICS OF ANTLERS

Two basic characteristics are important in the general approach to recognition and these must be clearly appreciated.

Firstly, an antler retains the general shape of its appearance from year to year provided that it, or its pedicle, has not suffered substantial damage. This means that although the number and length of tines, and the length and thickness of the beam, can undergo change from year to year, the general appearance and curvature form, in side or face-on view, remains similar (p 66).

Such similarity may also be traced from the male parent to a male offspring not unlike the similarity of features in humans of two generations.

Secondly, there are characteristics of antler development which indicate whether the antler should develop well or poorly. The most important are as follows:

1 As long as the antler formation is thick at the top there is hope for further improvement; when the thickness lies at the low part of the beam, improvement is unlikely. In red deer this thick area comes immediately under the tops; in roe it appears below the top fork; fallow show it by development of a firm palmation from the third head onwards, without deep 'incisions' into the palm.

2 In red deer, the antler which is in its second head or older can be inscribed into a triangle if it shows a poor future; an antler which can be circumscribed by a rectangle shows a good future (Figure 12). In fallow deer the existence of a spur or a long brow tine is a good characteristic, just as, in roe, long brows are a good sign.

3 An important indication of antler value in all three species, in the first head, is the length of the antler compared with the length of the ears: the quick rule is that the antler in the first head must be at least equal in length to the ears. At the same time it is not true that the first or even second head must be even or straight and should have no irregularities; indeed, small 'kinks' and thickenings on the antler indicate where tines will grow later.

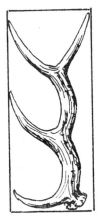 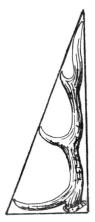

12 Shape as guide to recognition—red deer. An antler which can be inscribed into a rectangle is one with a good future, whereas one which can be inscribed into a triangle is unlikely to develop well

The illustrations which are included in this chapter will help to identify good and poor development of antlers.

Too often, also, accepted and widely held preconceptions concerning for instance the indications in antler formation turn out to be completely unfounded; for example, the notion that, if the top fork in a red deer antler is formed sideways on, it will never produce a crown, but a fore-and-aft one may do so. In fact, there is no guarantee of a crown either way. Finally, too often malformed heads are frequently shot because they are malformed, but without considering why the malformation has taken place and what the consequences of the malformation might be, especially in relation to heredity or to next year's regrowth.

All these problems need to be analysed and discussed because if it is our intention to build up a herd in terms of quality, these are important issues.

It may be helpful therefore to start with a brief summary covering the main species of deer and their respective antler development.

DEVELOPMENT OF ANTLERS

ALL THREE SPECIES

First head The young calf starts developing its first antler when it is about six to seven months old, and the growth of the first antler ends seven to eight months later, when the head is cleaned of velvet; the buck or stag has by this time just entered his second year of life.

Normally, not much should be expected of the first head by way of tines or shape; what is imperative is the length. The first head when cleaned of velvet must be at least the length of staggie's ears. The shape or spread at this age is of no consequence, and a straight and narrow antler is quite acceptable, whilst any tines must be accepted as sheer bonus. At fairly close quarters, an easy way of distinguishing the first head from older ones is that at this age the antler has no burrs (coronets)* and grows straight from

* For explanation of terms used in describing antlers see Figs 19, 20 and 21.

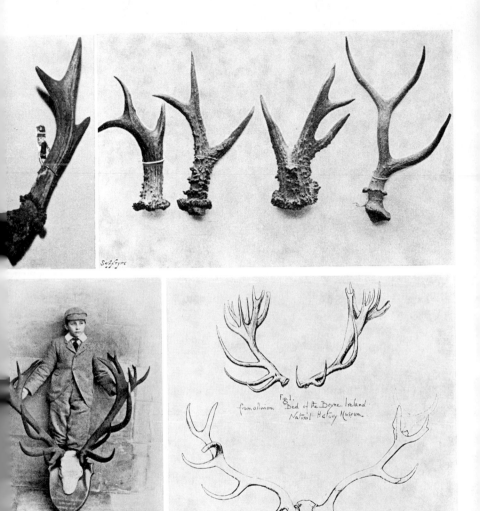

Page 65 (above left) Fossilised roe deer antler found during the excavations for Charing Cross underground station, London; *(above right)* four prehistoric roe heads found in Scotland, two right-hand ones fossilised (from J. G. Millais, *Scottish Deer and Their Horns*); *(below left)* prehistoric red deer head, approximately of present-day size but much thicker in the beam (from J. G. Millais, op. cit.); *(below right)* reconstruction of fossilised red deer head, 5ft span (Ibid.).

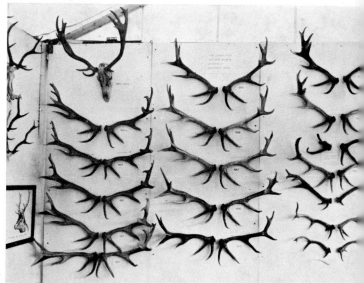

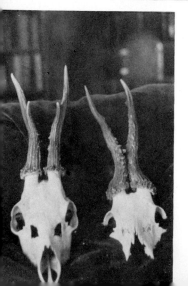

Page 66 The basic characteristics of antler reappear from year to year, provided that the animal, or the antler and its pedicle, has suffered no substantial damage. (*above*) The Endsleigh head; (*centre*) a Warnham blood head from Col Moncrieff's collection; (*left*) some characteristics of a head are inheritable; father and son's heads with very similar 'kink' in the right antler the pedicle, with barely a thickening showing at the bottom of the antler. This is an important characteristic for the purpose of distinguishing a good first head from poor subsequent ones; the absence of burrs is evident because the antler seems to 'grow straight from the head' whereas in the subsequent heads the thickening of the burr causes the hair surrounding the pedicles to form outwards growing tufts which can be fairly easily recognised.

RED DEER (Figs 13a and 13b)

Second head The second head begins to show a little more in the terms of quality. The length of the antler must be greater than in the first head, ie, must exceed the length of the ears by a fair margin. The brows should develop and should grow at a narrowish angle to the main beam; the top fork can also be noticeable. The brows need not be long, and if other tines do grow, the length of the upper ones should be at least equal to the length of the brows. The second head will produce a coronet (burr), thus a thickening at the base of the antler will be visible. Although in general terms one expects the length to exceed the length of the ears, in the event of the second head being a six- or eight-pointer this development may be accepted at the cost of the beam length. The tines need not be sharp or long, nor is their shape or indeed the shape of the antler of much importance. It will be noticed, however, that some of the shape characteristics of the second head will be repeated in the later antlers, spread for instance; a narrow second head may be an indication of a narrow spread in future.

Third head The third head should be at least a six-pointer. The shape of the beam should be well-defined; the length of brows is still of little significance, but the length of the upper tines is of importance—the longer the upper tines the better. It is also of secondary consideration whether at this stage the head has developed the top fork or a bey-tine; the sharpness or the shape of tines is still of no consequence, and the small thickenings on the beam or small 'kinks' in it spell nothing but good, indicating the inclination to grow more tines.

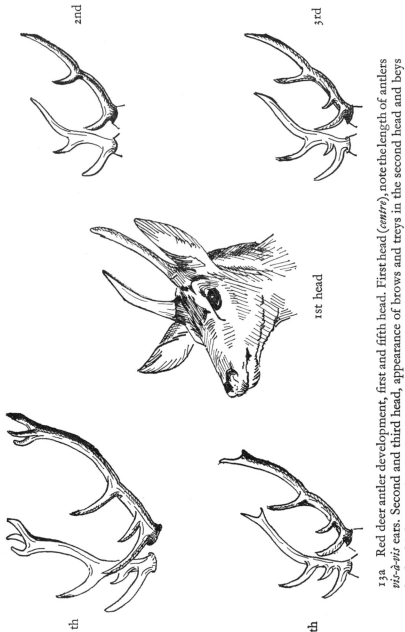

2nd

3rd

1st head

5 th

4th

13a Red deer antler development, first and fifth head. First head (*centre*), note the length of antlers *vis-à-vis* ears. Second and third head, appearance of brows and treys in the second head and beys in the third; note also thickening at the tip of the tines where fork (and ultimately crown) is about to form

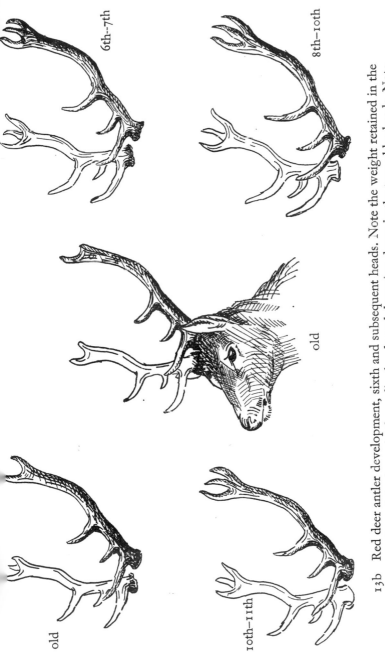

13b Red deer antler development, sixth and subsequent heads. Note the weight retained in the upper reaches of the beam in the earlier heads and dropping down in the two older heads. Note the blunting of tines and shortening of tines including disappearance of crown tines in the two oldest heads

What is important at this stage, however, is that the head should be inscribable into a rectangle (Fig 12) for the first time; the head which can only be circumscribed by a triangle becomes suspect unless it is very long.

It must be remembered that up to this stage of development the shape of the antler and above all the shape of tines are of little importance; sharp or blunt tines, thick or thin beam or tines, as long as they are not downright malformed, have no significance. *I have purposely laboured this point because it is at this stage, and possibly in the next head, that most errors in shooting are committed.*

Fourth head At this stage the tops must have a fork and the main tines should all be formed, so that the head should be an eight-pointer with brows, treys and a fork on top. The angle between the brow and the beam will probably start to open up; the brows should start to grow longer and curve upwards slightly at the tip, but their length should not exceed the length of the trey or the distance between the tips of the top fork.

The eight-pointer being the minimum fourth head, one expects certain characteristics which indicate the future: the antler should have its weight high up, the beam therefore becoming either thicker towards the top than it is at the bottom, or at least retaining equal thickness up to the top fork. A thickening below the top fork or, indeed, one within the top fork is a welcome sign, forecasting development of further tines at a later stage. Once the weight of the antler becomes concentrated at the lower part of the beam, the further development of the antler is unlikely, apart from the general thickening of the beam.

At this stage the absence of beys or a full crown at the top is not a sign of a poor head; on the other hand their presence is a definite sign of excellence. The general principle of the rectangular shape (Fig 12) applies.

Sixth to ninth heads These heads reveal the full development potential of the antler. At the sixth head the stag is most likely to have all the tines he is ever to grow. We could therefore expect the brow by now to be well developed and growing at an angle of about 90 degrees to the main beam and curving upwards at the tip; increase in the angle width every year, from now on, can be taken as a vague indication of age. The bey should be present, but its absence is not an indication of poor quality; the trey must be well developed, fairly long and sharply pointed; at the top the antler should have a crown, unless it has a bey. At the sixth head a ten-pointer head with brow, bey, trey and the top fork, or with a crown but without a bey, can be accepted as being a very good head.

Crown and eight-pointers (Fig 14 and pp 84, 133, 134) The formation of the crowns is normally preceded by a thickening of the antler at the top. That thickening may appear below the fork or in the tines of the fork itself; it often comes as a flattening in the upper beam, or one of the fork tines. Once the crown is developed it need not grow bigger every year; indeed, both the crowns and the beys tend to 'come and go' from year to year, the crown perhaps more so than the bey. Thus a three-pointed crown may become a four-pointed one, then revert the following year to three points, and the following year again revert to four points or even throw a fifth one. This is an important consideration. Often impatience plays its role in our approach to stags, and once we see a crown lose a point between one year and another, especially a three-pointed crown reverting to a fork on top, we tend to take this as a sign of going back. Normally these are phenomena of temporary regression, with improvement following an alternating-year cycle, ie, one year the crown is better, the next year it may be poorer, then better again. Once the deterioration takes place *for two successive years*, however, the head can be assumed to be starting to go back. In consequence, just because 'he carried a bigger crown last year', a stag is not necessarily shootable, unless he is an old one.

The six- and eight-pointer question is a complex one. When well developed, six- and eight-pointers are about the third and fourth heads of a normal stag. By well developed is meant a head with long treys and long tined tops; if beys are present with treys,

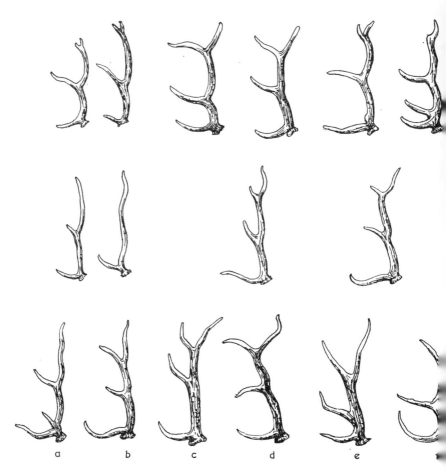

a   b   c   d   e

14 The 8- and 10-pointer; which is a good head and why. (*Top line*) good heads with long treys (inscribable in rectangle) second and third heads; (*middle line*) on the left, second heads perhaps just bearable (if they were older they would be bad), and on the right, older heads definitely triangular shape therefore bad; (*bottom line*) about fourth to sixth heads: (a) and (b) almost triangular, (c) weight low down, thin below top fork, (d) good tine formation but antler not nicely shaped, weight starts dropping down, (e) top fork starts too low, could almost be a trey and forkless top, (f) weight dropped low down. All these heads lack any indication of 10-point or better formation.

and the top fork is absent, the beys may be long or short, so long as the treys are at least equal in length to the brow. Normally such a formation will be accompanied by a fairly thick beam, either all the way up or at least in the upper parts above the trey.

When, on the other hand, the brows are long, the treys shorter and the forks on top very short or even absent, and to cap it the antler is thick at the bottom, becoming thinner towards the top, the head is a poor one. There is, however, an exception to this general rule when the beast carries his third and fourth head; if there is a 'bend' in the antler above the trey (normally slightly forwards, and then upwards again), such a bend indicates subsequent forking or development of a crown, especially when this 'kink' is also accompanied by a flattening on the surface of the upper beam or the tines of the fork.

Tenth head and older   Whilst it is known that heads deteriorate with age, it is not known exactly when the regression begins. As a general rule, however, the deterioration or 'going back' rarely takes place before the eighth or ninth year of life and usually about the tenth year. At the same time, we must remember that there are on record fourteenth and fifteenth heads still in their prime, and with no sign of going back. It has been suggested that there is a connection between the feeding and climate, or perhaps more likely the ability to feed and digest, and antlers going back: some deer, for instance, have harder teeth than others and therefore wear them more slowly—it would follow that they can chew and digest their food better and therefore can grow better antlers. But this is only a hypothesis and one not easily tenable when placed against the fact that, on the same ground, there can be a stag of twelve years going back, one of fifteen years showing no signs of deterioration, and one of the same age which apparently died of old age but with all his teeth still in adequate condition to allow him to chew and eat successfully.

There are, however, certain obvious signs of a head's going back; blunting of tines, shortening of tines, and their ultimate disappearance, be they the tines of the crown or others. The first tines to disappear during the early going back stage are usually the beys or those of the crown; accompanying this change is the characteristic thickening of the beam in its lower parts, from the coronet upwards as far as the trey. These changes do not always come on at the same time. One has to remember also that temporary deterioration can set in, as described before, and only a deterioration which lasts for two years or more can be accepted as a sign of going back.

The question which needs discussing at this stage concerns an old stag, let us say thirteen or fourteen years old, and there are such on the hill, which shows no definite signs of going back; is his shooting justifiable, regardless of the condition of his antlers?

The answer to this question must in practical terms be related to local conditions. After all, nothing is gained were the animal to die of old age during the winter; far better to gain the satisfaction of a good trophy well stalked! To alleviate any qualms one might have, it could be shot after the rut; an old beast like that can run itself very low in the rut, but may cover a hind or two. On the other hand, if in the early days of the rut an old stag (regardless of what his head might be) is found alone, without any hinds, this is a sign that he is either past his prime or indeed unwell and cannot master a herd any longer; he has to be looked at very critically.

What one is saying, therefore, is that if in a given area only a few stags survive until the age of thirteen or fourteen (without being shot, of course) then the old beast of that age can be, and should be, shot, preferably after rut. If, on the other hand, stags tend to live to a riper age without obvious signs of loss of condition, then one of that age should be allowed to go on. Whatever happens, we must prevent beasts dying of old age; they must be shot and their trophies secured.

ROE DEER (Fig 15a–15d)
Turning from red deer to roe deer, we shall find that there are certain features in the development which are familiar, even if some scaling-down in size may be needed.

15a Roe deer antler development. First head: (*left*) inadequate development; (*right*) good development. Note that where tines grow, length below that of the ears is acceptable; single spike, however, must be at least ear-length

15b Roe antler development. About second head: (*left*) inadequate
development; (*right*) good development. Note clear formation of tines,
rosettes and pearling

15c Roe deer antler development. Mature buck: (*left*) poor heads, thin, mis-shaped, inadequate tines or short tines; (*right*) well formed good heads

15d Roe deer antler development. Old buck: (*left*) heads tending to go back, note blunt tine tips, uneven length of antlers; (*right*) prime old heads

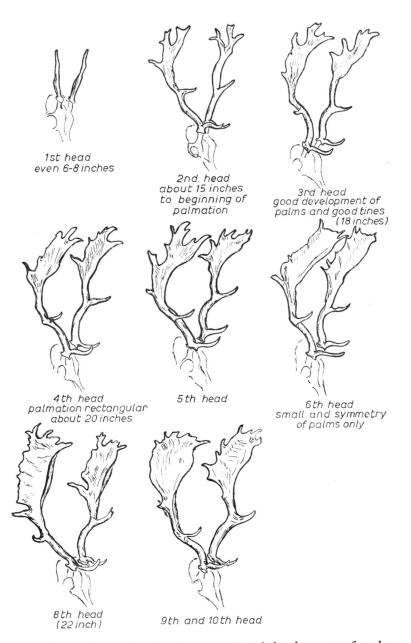

1st head
even 6-8 inches

2nd. head
about 15 inches
to beginning of
palmation

3rd head
good development of
palms and good tines
(18 inches)

4th head
palmation rectangular
about 20 inches

5th head

6th head
small and symmetry
of palms only

8th head
(22 inch)

9th and 10th head

16a Fallow deer antler development. Good development of antler,
first to ninth head

1st head
shorter than
6-8 inches

1st.head
uneven

2nd head
single spike
only

2nd. head showing
poor palmation
prospect

3rd head
poor palmation

3rd. head
triangular palmation

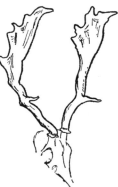

3rd head
uneven formation

3rd head
lacking brows

16b   Fallow deer antler development. Poor development of antler, first
to third head

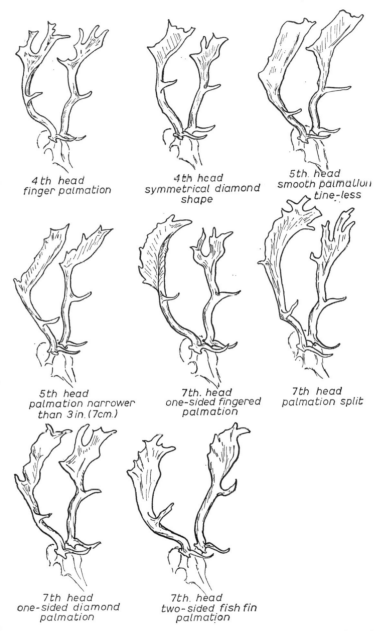

4th head
finger palmation

4th head
symmetrical diamond
shape

5th head
smooth palmation
tine-less

5th head
palmation narrower
than 3 in. (7cm.)

7th. head
one-sided fingered
palmation

7th head
palmation split

7th head
one-sided diamond
palmation

7th. head
two-sided fish fin
palmation

16c Fallow deer antler development. Poor development of antler, fourth heads and later

First head We have already discussed some of the characteristics of the first head that are applicable to all species. All that remains to be said is that a roe buck carrying his first head can hardly be mistaken for an older animal because he is still very much a fawn in appearance. However charming he may be, appearances must not sway our good judgement and, if the spikes of the antler are shorter than the ears, he is no good as blood stock unless the antler is exceptionally thick, or has a distinct fork on top or a brow point. The uneven length of the antler in the first head is of no consequence; thus one antler longer than the ears and the other slightly shorter is quite acceptable. A good sign of health of a young buck is late cleaning of his velvet and early change of his coat; the common belief that a buck still in velvet at the end of June must have something wrong with him is a fallacy. However, if the head is still in velvet in August, this may indicate some defect and shooting is therefore permissible. There is also a possibility of poor antler development accompanied by good body growth; this combination is unnatural and most experts advocate that the buck should be shot.

Second head The second head should at least be forked, by growing either the 'forward fork' of the brow and top or the 'top fork'. The antler should be more or less even in length and symmetrical in shape. The tines should be well developed, and the coronets should be well marked. One can also expect clear pearling on the beam, especially in those areas where good pearling is a local characteristic of roe. Needless to say, the stronger the antler the better. The coronets are important; they should form a definite and marked 'lip' round the base of the antler, and should 'curl' upwards at the edges. A drooping coronet on a young buck forebodes a poor future in antler development.

There is one exception to the rules set out above: a second head which is a well-formed six-pointer may be shorter than the ears, particularly if the antler is nicely formed.

Third head The third head should be a fully developed strong

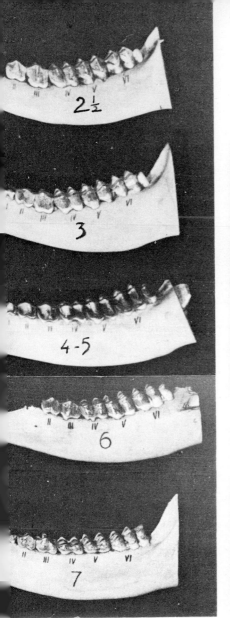
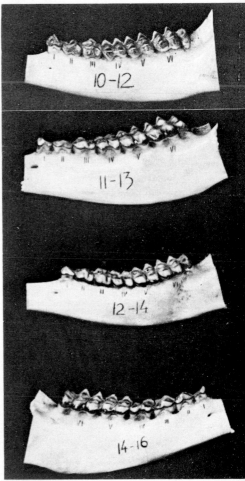

Gradual wear of the teeth enables us to establish the age of the beast. Note the differences between the wear of the third molar in the whole jaw photographs (hard dentine) and Fig 10 (soft dentine)

Page 84   Red deer recognition. (*above*) An almost 'rectangular' shape of head with the weight under the top fork; (*below left to right*), a young stag with bifurcated brow (in place of brow and bey) and a small crown on top; a side view of a good 10-pointer, which can also be seen head-on in the lower photo on p 133; a good enough 10-pointer which is unlikely to develop further (note the triangular formation and the antler weight centred low down); a good young head (probably second head with long brows and treys, short beys and fork on top)

antler of six points with well-formed and marked coronets and good pearling. The length is not always important and can be compensated for by thickness in the formation. Tines must be of good shape and the head symmetrical and well presented. The hitherto permitted lack of symmetry in the younger heads, or unevenness of antler, are no longer acceptable. A first-class head will have sharp points, good pronounced pearling at least half-way up the beam, and by now well-formed and thick coronets. Certainly a four-pointer head is unacceptable at this age, as is a thin antler without pearling.

Fourth head and later At this stage the buck enters the prime of his life, and whilst there may be premature signs of ageing in drooping coronets, the tines should be strong, long, and fine-pointed, and pearling should be distinct and heavy.

From now on, however, we can expect the head to start deteriorating. The first signs of this are the blunting of tine ends, the drooping of coronets and the gradual disappearance of pearling. The first tines to start going back are those of the top fork, but this is not always so, and old buck have been seen with the front tine almost vanished and the top fork still in good condition. It is difficult if not impossible to say more than that there is no existing rule which would help to establish accurately, or even approximately, when the antler is likely to start going back, and a perfectly developed ten-year-old buck is not an impossibility.

Whereas, therefore, deterioration of antler in a red deer stag indicates a good (if not advanced) age which may justify shooting, the same rule need not apply to roe buck. A good buck in good health, which has gone back early in life but which had a really good head, will probably produce good offspring although the early going back may be hereditary.

FALLOW DEER (Fig 16a–16c)
The perfection of fallow buck antler is in the formation of the palm, and the gauge of quality in the adult head is therefore based on the palmation. The early heads, however, have no palmation.

F   85

First head　As in the other two species of deer, all we expect of the first head is the length, which has at least to equal that of the ears. First heads which are more than spikers have been known, either growing a brow, or developing a flattening at the top with a possible beginning of future tines.

Second head　The second head is probably the earliest indication of value. It should have brows and possibly treys, and at least a flattening of the antler at the top. In very good stock, a spoon-shaped palm may develop with an uneven trailing edge. The total length should be somewhere between one-and-a-half and two ear-lengths.

Third head　The third head should bear fully developed brows and treys, each of not less than two to three inches. The palmation must be clearly marked by growing upwards from the previous year's 'spoon' and by broadening fore-and-aft. The trailing edge should start showing a number of rounded-off 'fingers', each of about half an inch in length; two of these should be more developed than the others, the bottom aft-facing spur, and the top fore-and-upward-pointing tine.

The palms should be fairly symmetrical and should not show deep serrations, although their existence at this age is not necessarily harmful. However, these serrations should fill in during the subsequent two years, to form a full palm on each side. The third head should also have a fairly thick beam below the palm.

Fourth head　This head is basically a development of the previous year's head with further improvements, and the point to note is that the serrations, if they existed in the previous head, should be filling out and not deepening. The most marked development is that of the brows, treys and spurs, which should be of good length and should start turning upwards.

Fifth head　Here the three tines—brow, trey and spur—must be fully developed; the palm should have well-developed fingers on its trailing edge, with the serrations no more than gulfs between the fingers of the palm.

Old heads At about eighth head one can expect signs of going back: the indications of the deterioration are the blunting and shortening of the spur, and the drooping and blunting of brows. The fingers of the palm become shorter and blunter. Like his cousin the roe, however, the fallow deer provides no rule as to when the going back is likely to begin; but once it does start, it continues, unlike the red deer where deterioration and improvement can take place interchangeably from year to year.

PART TWO

DEER MANAGEMENT

CHAPTER 4

DEER COUNTING

It is sometimes said that deer counting is an impossible task, or at least that it is bound to produce so inaccurate a result as to make it not worthwhile. The fact is, however, that, both in the dense woodland and in the open Scottish forest, deer can be and have been counted with sufficiently accurate results as to make reliable planning possible.

The approach to the counting of deer can be twofold and indeed should be so. In the first place, in a forest which is about to introduce systematic deer management, the initial concern is the overall number of deer and the breakdown between the sexes. Additionally, it is important to ascertain the number of calves, in order to establish at least the approximate rate of natural increase. These three figures provide the general guide and, related to the area over which deer roam, will also provide the density of deer on that area.

Secondly, the counting is an opportunity to establish the condition and age breakdown of the animals, thus giving a clearer picture of the general constitution and condition of the herd.

The first of these aims, the establishment of the overall numbers of males, females and calves, requires no great skill in recognition provided that the counting is done at a time of the year when males still carry their antlers and the calves are appreciably smaller than the hinds; it is also preferable to count when such ground vegetation as there may be has been cut by frost, thus allowing a clearer view of the beasts.

When counting is done with the aim of establishing total numbers, it must be done during winter months. The count is generally carried out by a number of people who move across the ground on a 'parallel course', usually into the wind, and who, whilst not necessarily in constant visual contact with each other, can survey each other's dead ground.

Moving forward over the ground on a predestined and agreed course, each member of the party notes or marks on a map the number of deer observed (making distinction between stags, hinds and calves, the time of observation, and, if the beasts are moving to an area covered by another member of the party, the time of the herd's disappearance. Similarly, the next counter will note the time of animals' appearance and the details of the herd, thus eliminating the possibility of double counting in the subsequent analysis.

Here, of course, a light portable radio transmitter/receiver, carried by each member of the counting party, can be invaluable, allowing for observation of all movements to be transmitted.

It is obvious that the amount of ground which can be covered is related to the number of counters available, the acreage and the type of terrain. It often happens, therefore, that the forest cannot be counted in a day without prohibitive use of manpower; there is no harm, however, in extending the counting over several days, but in so protracted an operation it is important not to disturb the beasts too much and to select days with more or less similar weather conditions, thus cutting down the possibility of local movements of the animals, for instance in search of better shelter. Of course with this method there is a chance of duplication; nevertheless, careful observation of the composition of herds, and accurate recording of types and sizes of animals, the direction of their movement and possibly the age groupings, may, during the final analysis of results, decrease much of this risk.

Some forests consider that a yearly counting is adequate, provided this is supplemented by observation during the rest of the year. There can be no doubt, however, that counting twice a year is safer, provides more accurate data and provides a better estimation of deer movements on the ground. The second count would ideally be done about three to four weeks after calving, which would not only allow for a double check, but would also give a better idea of the calving rate, before the winter takes a toll of the calves. Furthermore, a count at this time of the year provides a check on the animals just before the beginning of the stalking season, not unlike the last stock check before the start of operations.

The forest which employs stalkers or gamekeepers, whose job is mainly the management of game, may find that the feedback obtained from regular observation and throughout-the-year recording is adequate for normal planning purposes and requires a careful and organised count only once every few years. In such a case, in fact, the second aim of counting—the quality and age check of the herds—is continually fulfilled. Indeed, if the second aim is to be met by normal counting methods, the counters, be they employees or lairds, must possess the ability to recognise the quality factors in the beasts, an estimation which often has to be done as quickly as, sometimes more quickly than, it will be done whilst stalking; obviously they must record all their observations, and report and analyse their findings most carefully.

The 'quality counting' is an often-neglected task, yet one which is an important part both of selective shooting and of establishing a well-considered shooting plan, and one without which all attempts to improve the quality of animals are bound to suffer. The reason for this should be clear: the quality count gives us a standard against which the selective culling is decided upon. Furthermore, this is an opportunity to check upon the animals' age groupings and make appropriate allowances for age distribution of animals to be shot during the forthcoming season (see Chapter 8, 'Planned Management').

A method of counting, in some respects more efficient but requiring larger numbers of people, is one wherein a drive is organised, with the 'beaters' counting only the beasts which break back. A large number of beaters move downwind towards strategically deployed 'counters' who have to be quick in their recognition and recording, since a herd may stay in sight only for a short while, during which the finer points of the recognition have to be applied and the animals appraised.

In afforested areas, counting can be done by either method described above, but the most effective method is in fact by careful stalking without disturbance. This latter is easier than it would appear, because the established herds normally do not move away from their selected area where, under the protection of trees, they have cover and food.

If deer are being fed in winter, an effective method of counting is to note the number of animals visiting the feeding places once they have developed the habit of taking additional food provided. This method is particularly successful with roe deer, especially in winter when the snow is on the ground; at that time of the year, however, the establishment of roe's quality is obviously impossible, for the antlers have been cast and the new ones are still forming under young velvet.

TABLE 3

INDIVIDUAL OBSERVATION RECORD

Location: Date:

Weather: Wind: strong/medium/light N/S/E/W

Observation record:

		Sighted	Tracked	Direction of movement
Stags	Old			
	Medium			
	Young			
	Calves/Prickets			
Hinds	Old			
	Medium			
	Young			
	Calves			

Additional comments...

....

Recorded by:

Deer Counting

Many experienced woodland forester/keepers who have perfected their tracking skill swear by counting, going purely by the tracks of animals; to this end they are aided by the fact that, undisturbed, deer normally move along the same deer paths, and their skill allows them to make a distinction not only between male and female, young and old, but also to establish with remarkable accuracy the numbers in each group.

Of course, all counting will be only as accurate and reliable as the people who participate in it, and hardly ever 100 per cent accurate; the sole almost completely accurate method is by aerial photography—possibly only when the area is void of tree cover. This method entails not only considerable financial resources but also requires skill in the interpretation of the photographs taken.

Where the method of counting adopted relies on individual recording, be it during stalking or observation, it is useful to develop a standardised report form which is issued to the estate staff and used for all recording purposes (see Table 3).

If this method of recording is properly and diligently done, and the keepers visit the ground fairly frequently, it is surprising how accurate the summary (Table 4) of such observations can be, provided also that regular analysis is carried out. Such analysis is best done on the basis of each herd grouping, and it is therefore necessary to use one report record card for each herd spotted on each occasion and then to transfer the information from the report cards to the summary chart.

TABLE 4
HERD SUMMARY CHART

Area or Block:
Responsible keeper/stalker:
Record of herd observations:

		Stags				Hinds				Calves		
		1a	1b	2a	2b	1a	1b	2a	2b	m	f	Total
Herd (location	date: 12 Dec	2	1	1	3	6	1	–	2	2	6	24
and number)	date: 22 Dec	3	1	2	3	5	3	2	2	3	5	29
....	date: 5 Jan	3	1	2	2	5	3	3	2	3	4	28
	date:											
	date:											

(For explanation of terms 1a, 1b, 2a, 2b, see p 146-7.)

Each time the herd is spotted a record card is made and the summary updated. Needless to say, once the herd splits, new records have to be started; similarly, when the beasts split by sexes new records are needed.

Information collected in this way provides very good and accurate data upon which the movements of herds can be plotted, and stalkers (especially guests) can be acquainted with the ground and 'introduced' to the herds. Of course, initially this method may be found somewhat burdensome, but with practice it usually proves quite acceptable and very useful.

As deer management develops on an estate and becomes more sophisticated, so reliance on deer counting and accurate recognition increases. The importance of accurate counting, age and quality distinction will become more apparent in later considerations.

There is a final point which must be mentioned. It is very important that in all recordings animals found dead, for whatever reason, should be included. When possible, the reason for the death should be established; at any rate the animal should be aged, and, if it is a stag, the antlers should be recovered. To avoid double counting of the carcass, the safest method is to remove the lower jaw and attach to it a label describing the location, the reason for death and whatever other information is available, keeping this record with the records of animals shot during the season.

CHAPTER 5

DEER DAMAGE

There is no doubt that deer represent potential damage to both agriculture and silviculture; if coexistence between deer and man (who is, after all, interested in the protection of his land) is to be secured, then some means of compromise between their respective interests must be found.

Deer create damage for two basic reasons: either they are searching for food, or they have certain physiological needs which must be satisfied.

In the first case, deer damage will be related to the quality and quantity of food they can find in their allotted environment. It is a question therefore of the degree to which density is related to naturally available food which can be secured without creating damage. In the second case, it is a matter of environmental conditions which will allow the satisfaction of the physiological needs without undue damage to the economic needs of men. In both instances, therefore, there is a need for the creation of environmental conditions which are both acceptable to man and adequate for deer.

Furthermore, it is important to distinguish damage caused by deer from damage caused by other species. It is sometimes easy to blame the deer for the harm which rabbits, hares, moles, mice and even blackcock and capercailzie perpetrate, as well as that done by domestic stock. Where deer are mixed with cattle, sheep or goats, it is easy to forget that all of them can create damage, yet one does not shoot the stray sheep because it nibbled at trees, or the cow because it tore up roots in the field. The reason is that often a sheep appears to be of greater tangible value than a deer.

Frequently, young tree plants frayed or stripped low down are automatically assumed to be the work of a deer—and yet the work of a hare or rabbit, a mouse or mole, can look superficially similar. One must therefore ask the obvious questions:

> Why deer create damage;
> What has been done to stop it; and
> How important, or costly, such damage is.

But first it is necessary to analyse the type of damage which can be (or has been) done, and to differentiate between damage caused by deer in the field and in the woodland.

GENERAL CONSIDERATIONS

There are some basic points which should be considered when discussing damage caused by deer.

Firstly, deer damage is not, strictly speaking, an 'area activity'; it is rare, for instance, to find a large number of trees close to each other and all extensively damaged. The exception to this may be found when deer have been browsing in very young, unprotected plantations. In most instances deer select the trees which are, more often than not, weaklings, and which are suitably positioned, preferably being isolated; thus in close planting damage is less than in open planting. The supposition that prevention of damage in a plantation of several thousand trees is a mammoth task is therefore far from accurate. Granted, it may be difficult to select the right trees on which to place deterrents, but in fact even if all the trees to a depth of ten yards along the fringe of the plantation (where damage is normally concentrated) were treated, although it would be only a fraction of a large plantation area, it would cover the most vulnerable part of that area. Hence a spraying operation is usually confined to the peripheral ten yards.

Secondly, spraying in order to kill grass and other ground growth deprives the deer of the bulk of their natural diet, and thus encourages them to attack trees in search of uncontaminated food.

Thirdly, it is unlikely that, even under ideal conditions, all planted trees will survive for ultimate cropping. Deer damage is not, therefore, the sole reason for lack of total silvicultural success; furthermore, as mentioned above, deer prefer the weaker trees which in any case have a minimal chance of survival.

Fourthly, if deer are to be exploited as an asset and considered purely in terms of revenue from the sale of venison, they can provide a very reasonable income; compared with the income from timber, the income from deer recurs several times whilst the period of tree or forest rotation is, say sixty years. At a compound rate of interest, such revenue can be a significant item. For example, in the sixty-year tree-growing cycle, one could expect a turn-over of roe deer ten times, of fallow deer six times and of red deer four times: if the holding was 100 beasts, it would produce 50,000–60,000 lb of venison which, even at a conservative price of 20p per lb, can represent £10,000 to £12,000. This does not allow for letting for sport or income from possible by-products. Even so, the revenue quoted could challenge the value of tree damage, especially if one considers that trees are vulnerable only in the first 20–25 per cent of their life cycle.

Admittedly, the above considerations relate to woodland, and do little to cheer the arable-land farmer. He, however, can look to fencing and other deterrents, especially chemical ones, which will stop or decrease damage. Fencing in particular is worthy of consideration, for although its cost is high, it does qualify for a subsidy (at the time of writing) of 50 per cent of the cost and, of course, can be of lasting service.

DAMAGE CONTROL

The problem of damage caused by deer is often discussed, but all too frequently the method of approaching it is negative and the remedy suggested is, simply, the extermination of deer; a drastic, shortsighted and, to many, especially to nature conservationists, an irresponsible solution. It is a solution often contemplated, however, because the problem itself has not been properly understood and the economic value of deer has not been sufficiently considered or appreciated.

TABLE 5

SYSTEM OF PREVENTING DEER DAMAGE

Environmental			*Preventive*	
Decrease in deer population	Improved natural feeding	Additional feeding (artificial)	Care of plants or areas against: Browsing Stripping Fraying Threshing Rubbing	
			Area protection	*Plant protection*
			Fencing	Mechanical
			Spraying	Chemical
			Chemical and acoustic deterrents acting on Smell Hearing Taste	Mechano-biological

The field of anti-deer damage activity can be divided into two main groups (see Table 5): the first of therapy (repair to damage) and the second of prevention (prevention against damage). Therapy is a problem for botanist, farmer or forester, but prevention is the business of all those connected with deer.

OVERPOPULATION

Recommendations regarding the proper density of deer population are contained in Chapter 6; suffice it to say here that the density of population has a direct bearing on the incidence of damage, especially where the overpopulation is high (as it often is in Britain) and the quality and quantity of natural food is low. If one is prepared to accept this fact, then the advantage of maintaining the right level of density, in areas of high potential damage to agricultural and silvicultural economy, must be obvious. This is not to suggest that, with the correct level of deer population, damage will completely cease, merely that it should decrease to a level at which it is easier to control.

Deer Damage

FEEDING, NATURAL AND ARTIFICIAL

Accepting the threefold phenomenon that damage is (1) to some extent influenced by density of population as a result of (2) food shortage consequent upon (3) high density, it stands to reason that provision of food will have a direct bearing on the incidence of damage. But whatever the extent of liability to damage, there is always at least one method of overcoming it—either more or less comprehensive according to need or wish. Even a comparatively inexpensive dressing of the natural grasses will have good results. More sophisticated methods can be tried, such as planting small fields of additional food, sowing grass etc to improve environmental conditions, and possibly additional feeding, either with simple or complex fodders from hay, maize and other farm products, or with compound foods such as cobs and nuts.

Winter is the lean period for all game, and just as small game are normally fed by the owners and shooting tenants, so deer, especially in areas where snowfalls are heavy, should be fed. To this end a mixture of hay and dried clover, possibly some oats, if these can be spared, serves a good purpose. From the point of view of damage, artificial feeding will prevent, or at least decrease, stripping and browsing, the two actions which, particularly during a frosty winter, can cause considerable economic loss.

Hay and clover thus laid out should be fresh, not musty; musty hay can play havoc with deer's digestion. Normally deer will not touch old or rotting food, but if forced to do so by hunger will eat anything, with disastrous results.

FIELD DAMAGE

Needless to say the most vulnerable areas of cultivation are those adjoining a free range of deer habitation; there are also seasonal conditions which can change both the degree and the severity of the damage incurred. For instance, provided the ground is hard in winter, deer feeding off winter cereals do little harm and, in fact, may do a certain amount of good provided they cannot trample the cereal into wet soil. Once the ground softens as the

G

spring approaches, the animals must be moved from winter cereal fields. Conversely, in fields of roots, particularly beet and turnip, deer can be injurious at any time of the year until the crops have been gathered, for which reason some estates are prepared to allow deer on to agricultural land after the harvest, protecting only those areas which are damage-prone throughout the year.

WOODLAND DAMAGE

Damage to woodland is of a different character. Basically, all deer are fond of young shoots and buds; furthermore these present not only tasty, but in most instances fairly nutritious, material, especially as an addition to ground growth. It could be argued that the nibbling of shoots, even of the leading shoot, is not wholly destructive, for the tree will grow another which has an equal chance of producing good-quality timber, but it is bound to affect the speed of its development. Furthermore, one must accept the fact that continuous nibbling of the leading shoot will result in prolific side growth instead of upward growth, and the resulting formation will be that of bush rather than of a tree. This is most noticeable in the weaker planted trees and the tree seedlings which may well be destroyed as a result of their leading shoot being bitten off. This danger is greatest in sparsely planted woodland, where the inter-tree cohesion is low; furthermore, the tree-growth in sparsely planted woodland is slower, thus the exposure to danger lasts longer than in densely planted areas. These problems, however, seem to be greatly decreased in those places where a naturally regenerated and mixed forest is grown and where damage caused by browsing on shoots seems to be less dangerous to survival than in areas of artificial planting—possibly on account of either stronger growth, or a more plentiful supply of trees, as well as their normally greater typological mix.

A greater problem is caused by fraying and threshing, rubbing and stripping. Fraying, threshing and rubbing are done mainly by the male deer with their antlers, either whilst cleaning the antler of velvet, or whilst marking out their territory during or before the rut. Stripping is done by either sex, using their teeth to cut through the bark and to tear off strips by an upward movement of the head.

Clearly, deer are a danger to, and can cause havoc with, woodland areas, and, in considering deer management, these facts have to be taken into account; however, as with everything else it is important to retain a sense of balance and a sense of values—and additionally a sense of justice.

DAMAGE CONTROL IN WOODLAND

When considering the woodland deer, one tends to forget that whilst the deer may cause harm, they do also keep down much of the scrub, which otherwise—especially in plantations and self-regenerated areas—could stifle the growth of the trees; consequently some of the clearing work, which normally would have to be carried out by paid labour, is done gratis by the deer. In many instances, moreover, deer seem to attack the weaker saplings and seedlings, which in all probability would have died anyway. In any case, deer damage can be decreased by wise management and by a better understanding of deer matters. For instance, it is clear that a high density of deer will represent a greater potential damage than a low density, and yet the problem of deer density in relation to area is still not properly understood. Furthermore, whilst we are prepared to blame the deer for damage, we are not equally prepared to defend the woodland against the deer; yet it is not so very difficult, and with the right methods need not be very expensive.

The vulnerability of woodland is not static; it changes with age and is related to the origins of woodland, whether it is self-generated or planted. The most vulnerable woods are plantations, grown from seed or from young transplanted seedlings. This is attributed to the fact that transplants are weaker, and therefore softer, than naturally grown saplings. It is perhaps for this reason that the incidence of damage in naturally regenerated areas of woodland is much lower than in planted areas. The second important point is that damage tends to be lower in mixed conifer/

deciduous woods (planted or naturally regenerated); the denser the growth, the lower the incidence of damage.

Special planting or undersowing of deciduous trees in a conifer area, or the addition of good-quality grasses in rides, firebrakes, gulleys and narrow valleys (where trees are not normally planted because ploughing is difficult) will do much to reduce damage to the trees. Equally successful results can be obtained through the propagation of thickets among the plantations. Another system is to leave narrow strips of open land among close-planted conifers to encourage natural ground growth; there is no doubt that this method provides additional food, but, conversely, it allows deer into a more open area in which peripheral damage can be caused.

It is worth reiterating that deer will tend to attack the weaker, rather than the firmer growth. Finally, roe-damage to vulnerable leading shoots virtually stops when the tree is some four to five feet high, and red and fallow deer damage at a stage when the trees stand about six to seven feet high.

The problem is therefore a limited one—limited in time and environment—and much of it is, or can be, controlled.

DAMAGE PREVENTION

The diagram of deer damage in Table 5 (page 100) lists under preventive measures, mechanical, chemical, etc methods of damage prevention. These can be divided into two main groups—area protection and individual protection—implying either that an area is defended against deer damage, or that each tree in the area is treated against it.

INDIVIDUAL PROTECTION BY MECHANICAL MEANS

The only mechanical deterrent in area protection is glass wool, wisps of which are placed on the branches of trees in a 'Christmas-tree' fashion; but this is quickly carried away by the wind and washed down by rain.

Most of the mechanical methods of protection are those used in the protection of individual trees or shrubs. The principle is to protect the tree by such prefabricated devices as the 'spiked rod', the 'spiral', 'hoops', the wiring of trees, and the 'cuff', These methods will be self-explanatory from the illustrations in Fig 17. The expense of application very much depends on the ingenuity of the user. Ready-made individual mechanical deterrents are not manufactured in Great Britain as yet, but most of them are quite easy and simple to make and do not require an immense amount of material or skill, although a certain expenditure in man-hours is inevitable. These methods are particularly useful in combating such damage as stripping and fraying, both of which are often

17a Individual tree protection. A method of tying a conifer against fraying or stripping. When using this method some fraying may still be experienced on the outer layer of branches but this is harmless and negligible

17b Individual tree protection. A typical brush for application of deterrents

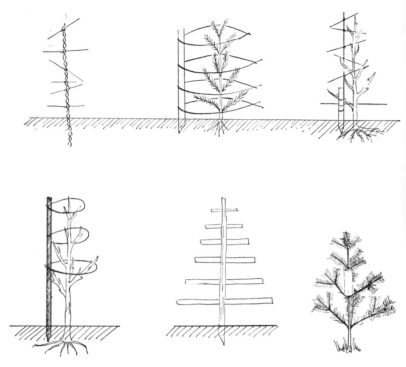

17c Individual tree protection. *Bottom, right.* A tarred paper or polythene collar preventing fraying or stripping on the main trunk of the
tree. It si important that the collar is placed exactly at the right height,
ie, at theheight at which damage occurs

17d Individual tree protection. A method of denying deer access to
the tree by using materials often found in the woods

17e Individual tree protection. A more elaborate method similar to 17d, but using other materials: (*left*) polythene sheeting, or straw; (*centre*) stakes; (*right*) wire mesh collar

confined to selected trees or selected small areas. Another type of damage is rubbing; mainly a habit of fallow deer, it takes place during the time when they change their coats, and the amount of damage thus inflicted is normally not very great. Area deterrents or individual deterrents may be used to keep the animals from those plantations where their weight is sufficient to break the young trees. The damage inflicted on old trees is normally small and of almost no consequence, especially when compared with the extent and value of other types of damage. On delicate or valuable trees, barbed wire can be used as a deterrent, loosely wound round the trunk.

Damage by browsing is an important point, especially in woodland areas and particularly when it concerns the eating of the leading shoots of young trees; the simplest method of preventing this is to attach a bit of paper, foil, wire or metal. Needless to say, the longest-lasting of all will be a metal strip or a wire collar; a few sketches of these are shown in Fig 17f. These methods are effective and, if made of durable material, should last not months but years.

Another form of damage which occurs in some areas is stripping, but this is a peculiar activity in that it is not widespread, and does not happen consistently; it starts without warning and ends abruptly. So far it has not been clearly connected with a particular shortage of food, a mineral, or similar needs. Apart from

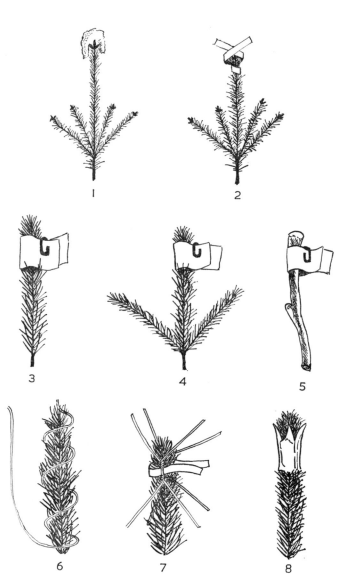

17f Protection of individual leading shoots. (1) glass wool strands;
(2) strips of tin or aluminium foil; (3–5) strips of paper and paper
fasteners; (6) wire spiral; (7) combination of wire and metal strips; (8)
thin metal crown. All these deterrents can be manufactured with ease
using materials found around the house (cooking foil, thin zinc-
plated wire, cut up food tins, etc)

chemical deterrents which are effective but usually short-lived, an increasingly popular method of prevention, especially in conifer woods, is to scar the bark with a sharp-toothed, comb-like implement or with a fine-bladed plane. The principle of this method is to make the tree 'bleed' resin at the height at which deer would strip the bark; the resin will then stick to the deer's lips and teeth, and this deters the stripping. The one obvious drawback of this system is the fact that scratching has to be done carefully, so as not to arrest the flow of sap under the bark. This method can be expensive in man-hours if a large number of trees have to be treated; on the other hand, if stripping is noticed at an early stage, and the newly attacked trees, or those in the proximity, are scarred, this will be an effective protection.

AREA PROTECTION

Fencing Fencing can, of course, be made in the orthodox way from timber, strands of wire or wire mesh. In the latter case, the chain link should be of wire not thinner than one-twelfth of an inch. Electric fencing is worthwhile only if a multi-strand fence is used, with distances between the strands which are too narrow for the deer to get between, and the topmost strand of which is high enough to prevent the deer jumping it. Also, a higher voltage is required than that used for sheep, cattle, or other domestic animals, making this system expensive.

Provided it is suitably constructed, fencing is the only fully preventive measure which can be taken.

In area protection, fencing is possibly the simplest method. Like fencing, other means of area protection can be expensive and may require considerable resources. The aim is either to fence in the deer, confining them to a given space, or else to fence in the area where we wish to prevent the damage, leaving the deer free outside it. In the first case, the fence must be made permanent, which is an expensive undertaking; in the second, a fence may have to last several years, after which it can be allowed to fall into a state of disrepair, or be moved elsewhere if suitably made.

Furthermore, temporary access to land may be allowed by

dropping a section of the deer fence thereby allowing access to cultivation and then driving the deer off the land and re-erecting the fence when the deer become 'unwanted'.

When using the first type of fence, it must be remembered that within the area of confinement the deer population must be of the desired density, and must have sufficient shelter, water and natural or artificial food to survive throughout the year. A deer's sense of hunger is very acute, and to satisfy it the animal will jump a fence or even break through it.

Acoustic deterrents   Acoustic deterrents, normally classified as area deterrents, consist of anything which makes a noise, hung along the edge of the plantation, and suspended semi-freely to encourage noise to be made at the slightest breeze. Tin cans with a weight inside are popular and effective—as far as this system can ever be effective. Before this method is used, however, its drawbacks must be considered. At a period of complete calm in the weather, the deer may get into the area thus safeguarded, and should a breeze spring up when deer are inside, they may be kept there for some time; for this reason, the method requires periodical inspection with a view to taking the 'acoustic fence' down and letting out any deer which may have got inside. In addition, should the deer be trapped inside during a gale, they are likely to panic as a result of the noise all around them and then to stampede, creating greater damage than they would have done in the normal course of events in an unprotected area.

Optical deterrents   Optical deterrents are basically similar in idea to acoustic deterrents, the difference being that instead of noise-making gadgets, strips of coloured rags or tin foil are used, or scarecrows placed round the area. This method is efficient for a short time only, since, as with smell deterrents, the deer will get used to the novelty; for this reason, the lines of optical scares should be moved from time to time.

Chemical deterrents   At the time of writing, chemical deterrents in Britain are still in the experimental stage, possibly because the market for them is so limited, and for this reason very little progress has as yet been made with home production. Owing to the expenditure involved in the importation of chemical deterrents, this system may have to be confined, for the time being, to the mixtures which can be easily and locally procured. This method of protecting a given area is based on the deterrent properties of certain chemicals, their smell or their taste, or both. The area is sprayed either throughout or along a peripheral strip, depending on the qualities and properties of materials used. Chemical deterrents can, of course, be applied to individual trees.

Protection by smell   So far, the greatest group of preventatives that have been experimented with are those which act on the animals' sense of smell. Both the home-made and the purchasable deterrents in this group have varying degrees of success, and varying methods of application. Quite recently a number have appeared on the British market and, having proved themselves successful, are slowly gaining popularity.

One must bear in mind that some of the chemicals may have

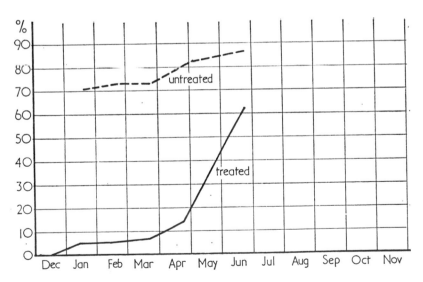

18   Browsing damage to terminal buds

a toxic effect, and the purchaser would be well advised to ensure that such an effect is acceptable.

Quite recently a number of deterrents against browsing by fallow deer have been tried by a group of landowners, with results as shown in Fig 18. After one application, the degree of damage decreased very considerably for a period of three to four months, after which time the weathering of the deterrent limited its effectiveness; this is one reason why odiferous deterrents have only a limited use. Also, deer become used to a strange smell and, after a time, will combat the fear which it generates in them and will return again to the feeding areas; the introduction of a variety of deterrents, therefore, is useful in the attempt to provide a lasting effect.

The deterrents recently on the market are Monacol, Silvacol 'A', Silvacol K, Cervacol, Fowikal, Runol, and FCH 60 I and TF 5. Some of these colour the trees, and some may be more toxic than others. If the maker's description does not adequately cover degree of toxicity to animals (the deterrent may also affect humans, even if not with lasting effects), a check on this point should be made.

The simplest and the cheapest among home-made deterrents is a mixture of 50 per cent manure water, 30 per cent whitewash and 20 per cent cow manure, well mixed and strained with a possible addition of 1 per cent creosote. This mixture, either painted or sprayed, is effective for a period varying from two weeks to two months, depending on the time of spraying and the amount of rainfall. It acts by means of its smell, which is repugnant to deer, and in later stages, when the smell has almost disappeared, may act through their sense of taste. Thus in the early stage it is an all-round deterrent, whereas after a time it is effective only against browsing.

In the same way, various industrial chemicals may be used, but care must be taken as some of the very efficient chemical deterrents will also kill plants or at least damage them, while others will not only keep away deer but also small game. A series of experiments has therefore been undertaken on the Continent to establish the degree to which chemicals can be used without noxious effects on other forms of life, and numerous firms have produced their own results in the form of manufactured deer-deterring mixtures. A list of these, together with explanatory notes, can be found in Appendix 1, together with some descriptions of applications and results obtained.

In general, the basic deterrent chemicals are coal tar, wood tar, secondary oil-refining produce, sulphites, resins, minerals and organic products.

From that multiplicity of chemical groups, Meyer, in 1939 (Ref 4), selected the following:

1 Carbolic; heavy lubricating oil; solution of copper sulphate.
2 Tar emulsion; emulsion of animal oil.
3 Non-soluble high molecular and thick hydrocarbons, ramified or neutralised through C, Br, CN, O, CO, SII, NO_2 or COOH.
4 Lower grades of petroleum products.
5 Fat acids which have retained their aldehydes.
6 Cattle fats; cattle blood; Vaseline; acid-free oils.
7 Technical benzol, chlorinated and mixed with water or white-wash.
8 Anthropin.

In practically all cases, these chemicals cannot be used undiluted and require additions in order to neutralise their harmful effects on various forms of growth; only very few can be used in their basic form. Most of them are applied by spraying or brushing on, or dripping from containers, thus forming an odour barrier. Furthermore, the more potent the smell (and therefore the more effective as deterrent) the greater is the loss of smell density due to evaporation, over a period of time.

Protection by taste A comparatively new approach to area protection has recently been developed and applied experimentally on the Continent, especially in Poland. This has come about because the hitherto-used preventative measures, based on chemicals which acted on the sense of smell, have been found to be too short-lasting for effectiveness. Up to now most of the chemical deterrents have been based on a combination of insecticides mixed with deer repellents; they were normally sprayed over an area or sometimes applied to individual trees, in the latter case being tar-based. However, the more effective the chemical, on account of its powerful deterring smell, the more short-lasting it was because of its aerating and evaporating qualities; at best, especially in the periods of wet or hot weather, its duration would be a few weeks. Furthermore, after a time a continuous application of smell repellents resulted in the deer becoming accustomed to the smell, to the extent that they disregarded it.

Consequently, the emphasis has been moved from deterrents by smell to deterrents by taste. The research effort was directed in two main fields—protection of the leading shoot on a tree, and area protection, by general spraying. It soon became apparent that whilst a deer will become accustomed to a strange and deterring smell, it will always avoid an unpleasant taste. The Institute of Forestry and the Institute of Game Research in Warsaw have jointly developed two deterrents, Repentol 1 and 2—the first for protection of conifers on the basis of individual tree protection at an early age, and the other for protection of older trees against rubbing.

The test experiments reveal that both are successful, not only when the repellent is fresh but also after a while when the animals 'learn' to avoid either the particular species to which the repellent has been applied or to avoid the area of its application. Particular success was met in applying the repellent to the leading shoot but allowing feeding on the side shoots, thus not limiting the feeding area as a whole, but at the same time effectively protecting the tree. Furthermore, the application of repellent to the leading shoot can be quickly effected at the rate of $2\frac{1}{2}$ acres, or 14,000 trees, per day.

The summary of experiments can be presented as follows:

1 The protection of trees is best effected by the use of taste, rather than smell, deterrents.
2 General application of taste deterrents over an area forces deer out of the area quickly and effectively, even when the application covers only a proportion of trees.

3 Repeated application is effective because deer continue to dislike the taste while they get accustomed to the smell.

4 Application only to leading shoots allows deer access to side shoots, and thus to a large amount of high-quality food.

CHAPTER 6

DENSITY

From time to time one hears comments such as 'I don't know how many deer I really have', or 'The Deer Commission counted my deer six years ago and I had x hundred heads, and I am happy with that number', or 'The more the better—after all it's all venison and the price is not bad—thank God'; sadly, only rarely is one told 'I have Y hundred, and the density is N acres per head.'

It would be interesting to know how many farmers would have a similar attitude to their domestic stock, specially those on a free-range farm.

Without wishing to give offence, either to the landowners who hold deer on their land or to many friends of all races and creeds, I would say that the attitude of some people towards deer is not unlike that of some primitive nomadic tribes who allow their domestic stock of goats and cattle to increase without control, or with inadequate control, simply as a matter of pride, or just un-thinkingly. The condition of the cattle and the effect on land and vegetation is of no consequence to them; hence the great amount of soil erosion in areas inhabited by some of these pastoral tribes. Only slowly do they accept the notion that it is beneficial to keep their herds lower in numbers but healthy and well fed, instead of having vast numbers of sickly, underfed, scraggy and barely alive beasts.

The comparison may be an exaggeration; but free-range Scottish red deer compare poorly in health and size with well-fed deer of Scottish origin that have been well looked after.

In some areas, especially outside Scotland, the landowners are perhaps fortunate that their deer population—even if on the in-crease—have better natural feeding to help them to maintain and retain body weight, health and the sort of condition that puts them amongst the best in Europe; but the question is whether this lucky state of affairs can continue. Why, for instance, is deer damage given more attention today than it was twenty or thirty years ago? There can be little doubt as to one reason: as deer increase in numbers, so the damage increases. A sensible approach to the problem would be to control the numbers in such a manner that one is in control of the situation, instead of being forced to undertake drastic measures when the situation has become out of hand.

What is required, therefore, is forward planning in order to avoid the necessity for emergency drastic action, which is inevitably difficult and dramatic, can be costly, and is more often than not uneconomical. Because, by its nature, the emergency action has to be hurried, errors are invariably made which, although not always irretrievable, are notable and often of lasting consequence.

There are only two ways of avoiding the out-of-hand situation; one way is to feed the deer, the other is to plan their density.

Planning of density is an activity which must take into account such factors as type of vegetation, the surface area of land open to deer, the size of the animals, geophysical conditions, the level of acceptable damage, aims regarding venison production level, antler size and value (to attract stalking fees), ability to feed artificially or to improve vegetation, competition with other animals on the range, etc. Unfortunately we have so far made little progress in Britain to establish the basic values of many of these factors, and where research has been done, and some data exist, this is mainly related to a particular locality, depicting the conditions applicable to a specific herd or group of herds. However, much of the new information available suggests that continental research is applicable to Britain, at least to a degree which allows us to gain some guidance from it. For a time, therefore, continental guides can be used without too much risk—certainly with less risk than comes of doing nothing at all.

The factual information on hand at present is extremely limited.

Density

Ever since the Red Deer Commission was established in 1959, it has been known that Scottish red deer number some 180,000, and that the densities in Scotland vary from 17 to 39 acres per head of red deer (Ref 5). However, knowledge concerning roe and fallow deer population, or the population of deer in England at all, is very scanty apart from some old data related to deer parks and a hitherto incomplete census conducted by the British Deer Society.

We know that the Scottish red deer are smaller animals, in both body and antler, than the red deer from Norfolk, Suffolk or the West Country, or even those originating from the Lake District. We also know that deer—particularly roe, sika and other non-indigenous species—are spreading and that, as they spread, so damage reports multiply. These facts are not quantified or sufficiently detailed and definite to be used in any serious formula, but as time progresses further information may be available to the point at which a complete picture could be put together.

For instance, D. Welch (Ref 6) relates damage by browsing to red deer density; in that study, density is established by dung deposits—the density of dung pellet groups over a given area. The formula or relationship is as follows:

$$\text{Rate of browsing damage on birch saplings} = 2 \cdot 97$$
$$\text{Rate of dung pellet groups per 100m}^2 \text{ per week} = 1 \cdot 09$$

The study suggests that at a level of 0·5 dung pellet groups per 100m² per week, damage is negligible and that such density represents a deer density in the area between 65·6 and 131 acres per head of deer. This is very valuable information, for two reasons; firstly it appears to be the first study of this sort in Britain carried out scientifically and with the sole purpose of serving the 'deer cause'; secondly, it supports some of the continental findings upon relationship between damage by deer and deer density. It is also worthy of note that as deer are fond of birch, one could expect the damage to birch saplings to be higher than that to many other types of vegetation.

ESTABLISHMENT OF DENSITY FIGURES

In spite of the fact that much research on deer density has been carried out in various continental countries, there are still vast differences of opinion as to the densities recommended. These differences can be accounted for by a variety of approaches and attitudes to deer problems, the variety of geophysical conditions and, above all, the different aims and methods. Nevertheless, whichever method or approach is adopted, none would support the density of deer as high as that in Scotland (17–39 acres per head), as will be seen later in this chapter.

There are other factors which have to come into consideration and have an important bearing upon the approach to deer density calculations and studies:

1. The origin of the forest. A naturally regenerated forest is by its character richer in undergrowth and stronger in tree growth and development, and in consequence has greater resistance to deer damage with a better recovery capability than an artificially planted forest.
2. Location. A forest bordering on pasture-land, to which deer have free access, allows for a greater density of deer within it than one which is fenced.
3. Geophysical conditions. Rain, and particularly snowfall level, is a very important factor because snow cover forces deer to browse on tree and other growth; thus in a high-snow-fall area deer density may have to be kept at a lower level than in a similar low-snow-fall area.
4. Feeding. A forest in which deer have been and are being fed as a matter of course, thus countering damage, can sustain a higher deer density than another where no feeding is done or where feeding is only sporadic.

Professor Müller (Ref 7) bases his theory of density to incidence of damage ratio on the level of damage acceptable to forestry interests; he finds that incidences of damage over an area, through browsing of 10–15 per cent, through fraying of 5 per cent, are acceptable. He bases this assertion upon the approach to tree survival where a pine or similar tree should survive 50 per cent damage because this species has a high recovery potential.

In his detailed working of density he examines the food potential of various species of trees and also differentiates between young and old trees, in that he classifies them by species and age and allots feeding coefficients to each age group (see Table 6).

TABLE 6
MÜLLER'S FEEDING COEFFICIENT

				Forest age			
	1–5	6–10	11–20	21–40	41–60	61–80	81–100
Pine ⎫ Larch ⎬	50–70	5–25	0	10–26	30–50	45–65	45–65
Fir ⎫ Red fir ⎬	40–60	40–60	0	0	0	25–45	45–65
Oak ⎫ Birch ⎬	60–80	60–80	35–55	50–70	55–75	55–75	60–80
Alder	50–70	15–25	15–25	20–40	20–40	45–65	55–75
Beech	40–60	0	0	0	0	10–20	20–40

Müller then relates the coefficients of species and ages of trees by percentages to the overall area of the deer-inhabited range. The outcome of his calculation is not vastly different from Ueckerman's (Ref 8). Table 6 is of particular interest, however, because it suggests firmly that in some types of woodland the value of natural food provided by the woodland's ground growth is very small. Müller then applies the Mottl formula:

$$D = \frac{A \times C}{R} \text{ where:} \quad \begin{array}{l} \text{D is the density value} \\ \text{A is the area covered by each type of growth} \\ \text{C is the coefficient for each type} \\ \text{R is the total area inhabited by deer} \end{array}$$

and subsequently applies the density points in Mottl's Density Points Table (Table 7).

TABLE 7
MOTTL'S DENSITY POINTS

Density points	Acres per head of red deer
above 100	100
91–100	122–100
85–90	176–122
41–84	273–176
31–40	500–273
21–30	600–500

In connection with this table a further stipulation must be made; that is, if other deer are present on the range with red deer, a conversion can be applied of two fallow deer to one red deer and four or five roe deer to one red deer.

Mottl (Ref 9) himself worked out a different method of estimation of density, relating the deer-inhabited area to the type of growth which provides the feeding base. He also provides coefficients which he then applies to his formula mentioned above, as indicated in Table 8.

Ueckerman (Ref 10) provides some very useful guides on the subject of density which he established after prolonged research, but I have seen a very much simplified method attributed to him which simply allows 100–164 acres per head of red deer, 25–123 acres to fallow deer and 22–82 to roe deer, moving within these brackets according to the value of naturally found feeding matter.

TABLE 8

MOTTL'S COEFFICIENT OF FEEDING VALUES

1	Area of bush	179
2	Grass meadows in old deciduous woodlands	78
3	Grass meadows in old conifer woodlands	65
4	Grass meadows in old mixed wood	66
5	Grass, wood clearings, heath	48
6	Meadows, cultivation and other feeding areas within the range	56

The Hungarian Government, which controls the forestry interests in that country, has officially established the following densities throughout Hungary:

190 acres per head of red deer
120 acres per head of fallow deer
50 acres per head of roe deer

A much more demanding method, one obviously established for 'playing safe', has been suggested by the author (Ref 11). It is based on a number of works from the Continent (Refs 12, 13, 14,

15). This method relies on grading deer habitat by quality of feeding potential, as follows:

Forest

Very good area An area of forest so graded is considered to be one which, as a complex, is not smaller than 15,000 acres, with small fields and meadows within it. The ground is fertile, allowing for luscious growth of deciduous and coniferous trees (or deciduous only); grass in the undergrowth is of the sweet variety; a good proportion of wild undergrowth is available. Fresh flowing water is available within the area and is easily accessible to the deer.

Good area A rather cut-up area of forest with a preponderance of conifers; a comparatively small quantity of flowing water; folding or mountainous land, few meadows and feeding areas; limited dense undergrowth.

Poor area Sandy soil; very dry or marshy land; heather and grass of the sour kind; little sweet grass (but heather and sweet grass form an area which may be considered as *good* if the two are mixed and the grass of the sour variety is in a minority); peat, conifers with soft mossy undergrowth.

Field and Moorland

Very good area Fertile, well cultivated and drained, with wide variety of crops; forest areas in blocks of 60–100 acres within easy reach.

Good area Mixed land, well watered, in parts covered with scrub or smaller than 60-acre copses; total area of the block less than 7,500 acres (scrub included).

Poor area Sandy soil, moorland, heather and dry grass in preponderance.

Having categorised the land, the densities which can be applied are as shown in Table 9. In the 'playing safe' policy negligible damage by resident deer has been the prime consideration, and no other preventative methods have been contemplated.

Ueckerman has been mentioned before. His method of establishing deer density is too important not to be described in some detail.

His calculation of the optimum figure for deer density is based on Professor Nusslein's method allotting a figure value to such items as the type of afforestation and its surface area, its bordering

TABLE 9

'PLAYING SAFE'

Density Table

	Acres per head of deer		
	Forest	*Field*	*Moor*
Very good area			
Red deer	250	*	300
Fallow deer	125	300	*
Roe deer	50	150	100
Good area			
Red deer	500	*	400
Fallow deer	175	400	*
Roe deer	80	200	200
Poor area			
Red deer	750	*	500
Fallow deer	250	600	*
Roe deer	150	300	300

* Unsuitable for this deer.

TABLE 10

UECKERMAN—CULTIVATION POINTS

1 *Percentage of forest within the area*

%	pts
0	7
1–20	8
21–40	11
41–60	13
61–80	16
81 and over	18

Percentage of meadows within the area

%	pts
0	9
1–4	10
5–10	13
11–20	17
21 and over	22

2 *Geology*

Sand downs (diluvium, alluvium)	14
Red sandstone	20
Basalt, quartz	23

Shell lime	35
Glacial deposits	18
Granite	20
Oolitic limestone	30

3 *Afforestation*

Spruce, over 50%	pts 10
Mixed forest (at least three types of tree at 10–50% of area, each	15
oak up to 30%	15
oak up to 40 %	18

Pine, over 50%	pts 13
oak up to 50%	21
oak 60% and over	25

with other types of land, and the geology of the terrain. Score points are then applied which are translated into recommended density figures (Table 10) for the area of 1,000 acres.

Points appropriate to the area by its characteristics are totalled and land grading is arrived at as in Table 11.

TABLE 11

LAND GRADING

Very good areas	71 pts total
Good areas	61–70 pts
Medium areas	51–60 pts
Poor areas	41–50 pts

According to the 'goodness' grading of the area, the deer density is read off from Table 12.

TABLE 12

DEER DENSITY

Points Score	Roe deer	Fallow deer *	Fallow deer †	Red deer
40–45	6	4	8	3
46–50	8	4	8	3
51–55	10	10	14	4
56–60	12	10	14	4
61–65	14	14	20	6
66–70	16	14	20	6
71–75	18	20	28	6
76–80	20	20	28	6
81–85	22	20	28	6

* The first column refers to those areas where the fallow deer are denied access to agricultural areas; the second column indicates free access to the surroundings of the forest.

† Where it is intended that deer should not have access to the surrounding areas of agriculture, the figures representing equated values in respect of fields under cultivation (Table 9) should be excluded from calculation.

None of the figures quoted can be considered as absolute; they can vary by as much as 30 per cent.

CHAPTER 7

FEEDING AND SHELTER

In *Wild Deer* I have given a fairly detailed account of the results of early feeding experiments, conducted in the Schneeberg enclosure in 1930–41. The Schneeberg experiment is an important stage in the field of systematic approaches to deer improvement, using both new blood and balanced feeding.

The important facets of the Schneeberg experiment are those which indicate that an addition of calcium and phosphoric salts in a ratio of about 1 : 1 for stags, and an addition of easily digestive albumen for both sexes, produce excellent results. It was found that deer in coniferous woodland did not have the same opportunity for full body and antler development as those in deciduous woodland unless additional feeding was given to them.

When, as a result of World War II, additional food was decreased in both quality and quantity, a reaction to change was noticeable in the antler size of deer, which were nevertheless carefully looked after; the young stags of Schneeberg carried eight to ten points in their first head, and royals in the second head were not uncommon. There are experiments carried out in Britain today which prove that with dietetic additions it is possible for randomly selected hill calves to develop a six to eight pointer first head, on a 9–11 stone body, at the age of about ten months.

Before discussing the additional feeding of deer—its merits and disadvantages—some factual information from Schneeberg (see Tables 13 and 14) may be of use.

The Schneeberg results were achieved by carefully balanced diet arrived at by additions to food, with selective shooting. There is little to support the suggestions, sometimes levelled at

TABLE 13

CROSS SECTION OF SCHNEEBERG STAGS

Age (years)	First generation Number of tines		Second generation Number of tines	
	Poor heads	Good heads	Poor heads	Good heads
3	10	14	12	19
4	9	17	14	24
5	14	18	15	24
6	14	20	17	27
7	15	20	17	29
8	15	26	17	26
9	15	22	17	28
10	14	23	16	33

TABLE 14

DEVELOPMENT OF HEADS OVER YEARS RELATED TO
DIET FLUCTUATION

Age	Year	Antler weight (kg)	Antler length (cm)	Mean circumference of beam (cm)		No of tines	International points score
				Lower	Upper		
2	1933	3·35	88·5	14·1	12·3	11	155·6
3	1934	5·07	95·3	16·7	14·4	13	176·8
4	1935	7·64	116·4	17·7	15·1	14	201·0
5	1936	9·55	113·4	19·7	16·0	17	216·3
6	1937	10·18	121·0	19·8	16·2	17	222·1
7	1938	11·00	127·7	21·5	17·2	17	240·5
8	1939	11·00	130·5	22·0	18·0	19	247·0
9*	1940	10·50	126·5	22·2	19·0	20	234·0
10†	1941	12·00	117·0	22·0	18·0	16	225·2

* First year war-time diet.
† Second year war-time diet.

the administration of the experiments, to the effect that importation of new blood had much influence on the quality of deer; on the other hand, overwhelming evidence exists to show that a balanced diet of calorific, vitamin and chemical values, provided in easily taken and easily digestible form to allow maximal assimilation, was of major influence. To this end the following guide-lines were accepted:

1 Hay and other dehydrated fodder allows for 50–60 per cent absorption of mineral contents.
2 An admixture of minerals has to be supplemented to provide adequate mucol intake.
3 Stags need additional feeding during antler formation, and hinds during gestation and lactation, at the following approximate rates (per day):

Calcium (CaO)	2 oz
Phosphate salts (P$_2$O$_5$)	1½oz
Albumen	1·3lb
Nitro-free substances	4lb
Overall	8–11lb
Vitamin D	4,000–6,000 units
Vitamin C	3 grains
Vitamin A	0·1–0·2 grains

These figures can be compared with some provided later in this chapter and adjusted for size of Scottish deer. Furthermore Appendix 2 provides some guidance on the breakdown of some types of fodder.

Today, some thirty years after the Schneeberg experiment began to deteriorate on account of the war, we have similar guidance from experiments conducted in this country which prove the effect of feeding even when applied to the much maligned Scottish deer, the 'smallest and weakest' of the red deer. Body and antler can be improved out of all recognition (Ref 17).

FEEDING, NATURAL AND ARTIFICIAL

We must not lose sight of the fact that the male of the species, during a period varying from 120 to 190 days each year, must devote an enormous proportion of the vitality acquired from food to the rebuilding of antlers. To no less an extent, the female of the species, during the period of gestation and lactation, requires considerable quantities of food, admittedly of different chemical constituents, for her own sustenance and that of the born or unborn young. In a word, they must feed and must feed well.

A stag, to produce a head of antlers weighing 12–20lb, must derive from his food some 3½lb of calcium as well as 3–5lb of phosphorus during the period of antler-building. If we reduce the antler size to the Scottish size of 10–15lb, the proportional reduction in calcium and phosphorus would be about 2·8lb and 2·5–4lb respectively.

Hinds, during gestation and lactation, require $\frac{1}{4}$lb albumen, $\frac{1}{30}$lb calcium and a similar amount of phosphorus *each day*.

Table 15 represents the daily feeding requirements of red deer. The requirements are for stags weighing approximately 300lb live weight and hinds of about 240lb. In areas where weights are higher or lower, the total consumption can be increased or lowered in direct proportion, as shown in Table 15 for the average weights of Scottish deer. One must remember, however, that as we are aiming at increases in body and antler weights, increased amounts of food must be allowed for before the increases in body weight will occur.

TABLE 15

FOOD REQUIREMENTS

		Dry substance (lb)	Nitro-free substance (lb)	Digestive albumen (lb)	Total fresh food (approx) (lb)	Dry food content (lb)
Stags	Large	6–8	3–4	0·3–0·5	22	14
	Scottish	4·5–6	2·25–3	0·22–0·4	16·5	11·5
Hinds	Large	4–7	1·5–3	0·1–0·8	13	7
	Scottish	3–6·25	1·1–2·25	0·1–0·6	10	5·75

Note The lower figures for hinds shown in the table are those necessary for uncovered hinds; the higher figures are for the period of lactation. Hinds in gestation require a quantity approximately half-way between these two figures.

By his digestive and hormonal reproduction, the stag or buck builds up his antler; the chemical composition of it is shown below, to emphasise the need for balance in the diet (all figures are percentages).

H_2O	—9·7
CaO	—28·37
MgO	—0·6
Na_2O	—0·7
K_2O	—0·1
P_2O_5	—22·4

CO_2	$-3\cdot0$
SO_3	$-0\cdot3$
SiO_2	$0\cdot03$
N	$-5\cdot8$
Nitro-free substances	$29\cdot0$

It will be seen that unless the feeding conditions in the deer forest are such that the chemical components can be found, and then in sufficient quantities to meet nature's requirements, the deer will be forced to find these components somewhere, somehow. This they will do by raiding the agricultural areas in the neighbourhood, where most of their needs can be satisfied; it goes without saying, therefore, that they will inevitably damage the useful plants of the field or forest. By now it will be obvious that some of the damage is bound to be the result of the animals' search for what nutritionists would call a balanced diet. In order to prevent that damage, therefore, we must attempt to balance the deer's diet artificially to make available the elements they naturally crave.

However, no matter how much food is provided for deer, by nature or by man, some damage must be accepted; an idea of the influence of feeding upon damage can be derived from Table 16. The figures relate the damage intensity in the total crop of the forest using as a 'unit' one pair of deer in an area of 250 acres and where no damage prevention activity, other than supplementary feeding, was undertaken.

TABLE 16

COMPARISON OF THE INFLUENCE OF FEEDING UPON FOREST DAMAGE

	Coniferous (%)	Mixed (%)	Deciduous (%)
Wild forest—no additional feeding			
Browsing	5–7	1–3	0·3
Stripping/Fraying	5	2	0·2
Wild forest—with additional feeding			
Browsing	1–3	below 0·1	
Stripping/Fraying	1–2	below 0·1	

The provision of necessary additions to the deer's diet can be effected in two ways: firstly, and in some respects preferably, by the introduction of small fields each of a quarter to half an acre in size, arranged in suitable locations (often unsuited for other purposes), often found along the edges of gullies, or within the wide forest rides, and sown with a mixture of suitably selected crops which will attract deer and provide them with their needs, at the same time possibly diverting them from tree plantations and fields of high value; secondly, by providing fodder, fresh and dry, at times of need—often a difficult undertaking on account of transport difficulties during the winter months. An added advantage of either type of feeding is that if it is thought advisable to move deer from one area of forest to another, by rearranging the feeding fields or feeding troughs or ricks over a period of time (years rather than weeks) deer can be persuaded to move to the area where they expect to be fed.

Some suggestions as to crops and dry fodder which can be used will be found in Appendix 2.

It is difficult to produce an abstract example of a diet; it is thus advisable to investigate the feeding matter deer are seeking, and, by consulting the table of chemical contents provided in Appendix 2, to adjust the feeding matter provided. On the whole, such crops as grass, clover, wild rye, buckwheat, potato, turnips, beet, lupin, lucerne, sweet corn, and fruit-bearing bushes and trees will normally produce the required results.

THE PROPRIETY OF FEEDING

Feeding of wild animals is a question upon which there are many disagreements, of principle and method. As to the principle, some people feel that wild animals should not be fed and then stalked or shot; feeding is a method of taming, and through feeding the animals become at least partly tamed and therefore an easier sporting prey; furthermore, the animals may lose the ability to fend for themselves, especially during bad weather.

As to the method, the arguments and disagreements vary. There seem to be two schools of thought, the first of which considers that 'a little of what you fancy does you good'; thus they feed with whatever the deer will take with ease. Maize is one of the most popular items, because it is easily taken by deer and is often used to attract deer to the feeding places, often being successfully mixed with crushed or whole cobs or nuts to make deer take the latter more easily. By itself, maize is not a bad fodder, but it tends to produce fat, therefore weight. Thus, in producing venison for the market, maize will improve weight as long as the animals are not producing excessive fat. As for bone and antler formation, maize does a little good, so that the theory that a big body produces bigger bone and antler is only partially true.

As opposed to the policies and intentions of the 'maize school', there are the policies of the second school, often regarded as the 'scientific' school. Their approach should be understood with some ease by farmers. A farm stock diet is adjusted to meet the farming objectives; a porker is fed on a different stuff to bacon pig, a milking cow is given a different nourishment to one bred for beef; the tastes and likes of the animals play a secondary role in the diet provided.

So with deer, but with a difference. No animal except the deer family sheds its antlers and re-grows them every year; this in itself is an effort, and if we wish to help their effort, and ensure that the beasts have access to food they need, in order to give them the balance of diet leading to better and stronger body and antler, we may have to supplement the diet, even artificially.

Furthermore, we must try and ensure that the food available to deer is converted at the optimal rate, and if needs be assist that conversion. For instance, in winter deer take food of high cellulose content which requires breaking down by means of high fermentation to extract glucose at a rate faster than the natural process allows for. This process can be accelerated by an addition of urea, which will allow the animals to make better use of natural food taken. This is of particular importance during the winter when deer are forced to eat woody substances, such as heather, half-dry twigs etc because of the absence of more succulent food; it is also more important to moorland deer than to woodland deer who on the whole fare better. The right balance is achieved by means of increasing rumen ammonia, by giving the deer urea in block or crystal form; in most instances, however, some taste agent has to be added to incite the deer to take the otherwise unpalatable urea, hence some additives are added in the block form, or crystals could be added to the maize or other strong-tasting fodder.

One might say that additional feeding, for whatever purpose and with whatever aims, upsets the natural life of the animals, but this is the consequence of the already existing disruptions of the deer's environment created by man.

The question is not simply whether one ought to give deer marginal aid to help their natural digestive process; it is a matter of greater import—namely, should one supplement the deer's diet at all at time of need, and will such supplement represent in the first place an economical proposition, and, in the second, be considered in any way detrimental to sport, to nature as a whole, or to deer in particular?

There can be no doubt that, especially in winter, supplementary food will result in antler improvement in the male, better mothering in the female, and increased body growth in both. Furthermore, because they have an efficient metabolic system, the rate of food conversion is greater than in most other animals. One can therefore assume that, in the sense of conversion of unit value of food to unit value of venison, bone and antler, the conversion rate is high—even if, through the shedding of antlers every year, a proportion of that value is, in terms of revenue, wasted until the animal is killed. On the other hand, an improvement in the form, size and shape of the antlers is of value as an attraction to a sporting tenant who, at least from time to time, wants his 'royal'.

Further interest and encouragement with regard to feeding should be increased as a result of a variety of experiments on the deer's food conversion rate, all of which suggest the deer's ability to convert food taken into body material at a greater rate than any other wild or domestic animals. Needless to say, the metabolism will depend to a large extent on the existence of convertible food

Page 133 Red deer recognition. (*above*) A good 10-pointer with sideways-on top fork (developed a full crown next year, see top picture, page 151); (*below*) two young stags: (*left*) long brows, short beys, treys and small fork with the weight; (*right*) note the long tines and a well-developed top on both sides

Page 134 (*above*)   A collection of good stags. (*behind*) Very young stags with good heads; (*foreground, left to right*) a rectangular 8-pointer (needs watching as the weight of antler seems to be low down); a nice young royal—probably about fifth head; a very pretty 11-pointer of mid-years; (*below*) Stags of two age groups: (*left to right*) probably second head which will probably improve; a nice 10-pointer with large fork on top (probably third or fourth head); good quality 10-pointers, with the weight still high up the beam (both about fifth/sixth head)

and the rumen function of the animal, whilst the limits of conversion are set by the volume of the first stomach as well as the quality of food. Hobson (quoted in Ref 17) adds that the rumen activity will depend on the ability of microbes in the rumen to break down the cellulose chains into glucose, which can be freely fermented and burned in the body; for this purpose he recommends an addition of urea, to increase the rumen ammonia, thus encouraging the growth of bacteria which in turn help to break the winter intake of high-fibre food such as heather, twigs and bark.

Frahne's experiments and those of many others suggest that, as a result of the high metabolism of deer, changes in their diet can have quick and far-reaching effects (either improvement or deterioration). The changes can therefore be quite dramatic if, in a normally poor food area, good quality food is added, or if, after feeding deer for a time, the additional food is denied.

At the same time we must remember that deer, whilst not over-particular as to what they eat, will become used to poor-quality food, provided the demand for bulk can be satisfied. In this case, however, the high cellulose content often remains unbroken unless rumen activity can be stimulated.

The adjustability of deer to the environment is proved by deer of one area becoming quite fond of (or at least used to), foodstuffs which deer in another area will not touch, having access to more easily digestible materials. Examples of such are mosses, ferns, reeds, irises and rushes, bog growth, etc which Scottish deer will eat and many other deer will not.

Bubenik (Ref 18) quotes the roe deer's ability to convert food into bone and antler building substances; roe, he says, have the same absorption coefficient for inorganic and organic phosphorus and calcium, both during the body and bone development periods of early age and later, during the antler-forming periods. Once the body is fully grown and the bones fully developed, the inorganic minerals are not as easily absorbed as the organic ones taken through plant life with food; but the high rate of absorption and conversion from organic and inorganic sources returns each year at the time of antler-forming.

I

When talking of additional feeding, one tends to think primarily of Scottish red deer, mainly because those deer often live in poor feeding areas of the hills, whilst the roe and red deer outside Scotland, being woodland dwellers, find better-quality food. On the other hand, the roe buck too has to grow antlers, during the winter months, and in consequence needs just as much help as the red deer, especially when living in poor-quality woodland areas, such as coniferous woodlands; hence, poor roe heads in coniferous areas are not uncommon.

The problem of antler-building must be considered as an annually recurring short-term exercise, lasting three to four months and resulting in a build-up of bone formation which comprises between 10 and 15 per cent of the weight of the animal's skeleton. If, therefore, supplementary feeding is to achieve its objectives in relation to any deer of either sex, it has to be a positive action, carried out regularly and to a natural conclusion, ie, it must start at the time when quality and quantity of food naturally found decreases and must be sustained until the beginning of spring.

To achieve our complex objectives, there are several acceptable methods of feeding.

FEEDING COMPOUNDS, ADDITIVES, ETC

If the method proposed is that of placing food in designated areas frequented by deer, it ought to begin soon after the early frosts. Ideally one should start with food which deer will take easily and naturally; thus beet, turnips, hay, maize, etc are all good and adequate.

As soon as the deer have started taking such food, additions can be mixed in—minerals, including salt, urea cobs of crystals (the former preferably crushed), mixed with small grain or cut-up roots to start off. As the winter progresses, cobs can be increased and the other matter decreased, cobs being a compound of high food value.

Ideally, the food should be placed in troughs and under cover, to protect it as much as possible from climatic influences. This is an important aspect, not only because wet food will deteriorate, but also because deer taking wet, musty or fermenting fodder can be seriously affected.

Where deer are timid, the introduction of food troughs, ricks or shelters has to be done gradually, introducing ground troughs (often car and tractor tyres cut in half), with small quantities of food, and, after the deer have started frequenting the feeding locations, placing roofs over the troughs and ricks. Once feeding shelters of this sort are established, they can be left standing from year to year as deer become accustomed to them. A point to bear in mind when erecting such shelters is that the roofs should be either thatched or made of timber, rounded off at the edges so as not to damage the antlers when they are soft in velvet (corrugated metal, unless well-edged with rounded timbers, should not be used).

FEEDING FIELDS AND AREAS

If it is decided to establish areas of additional grown food such as turnips, beet, even grasses or clover, the deer should be allowed access to these in early winter.

Ideally, small troughs should also be used to provide the necessary mineral additives following the same pattern as established above. It has to be remembered that, in high concentrations of deer, small fields will be used up quickly—therefore sequences of them may be required, each one fenced and with a part of a fence capable of being dropped to allow access. Where calves have a winter survival problem, it may be found useful to allow only calves access to these feeding fields, by constructing part of the fence from vertical stakes and horizontal wires, the stakes being spaced wide enough to allow calves through, but keeping hinds and stags outside.

A word here on the subject of new woodland plantations. It has often been found that small areas, only marginally suitable for tree planting, can be adequately prepared to allow for sowing or planting of additional food. Even clusters of completely wild scrub often help. Above all, in many areas some grass and soil dressing can provide a considerable improvement of natural vegetation.

SHELTER

Deer react to climatic conditions probably just as much as to feeding, and shelter in adverse weather is of considerable importance. The woodland deer finds shelter in its natural surroundings. Scottish red deer in extremes of weather seek shelter behind rocks and crags, in narrow gullies and streams. This sort of shelter, however, does not provide the deer with adequate conditions for good development, and barely meets the minimal requirements; it probably does no more than save the animals from death by exposure. For this reason, there is a growing tendency to allow deer access to woodland once the trees have grown to an age where deer damage is only a limited and acceptable risk.

CHAPTER 8

PLANNED MANAGEMENT

The need for deer management has its origins in a variety of historical events and an equal variety of aims. Among these the first is the effect of human civilisation which disrupted the balance of nature in two ways—by the introduction of human requirements for land and by upsetting the balanced constitution of natural fauna; the second is the need to preserve nature for the sake of posterity; the third is that, being a sporting asset, nature needs husbanding and care to provide an acceptable level of economic return.

Whichever aspect is taken as a basis for management, it is necessary to ensure that the number of animals is related to the size of habitat and food available, and that this relationship is maintained; that the composition of stock is such that it thrives and is maintained at the optimum health level; and that stock can provide its owner with an economic return of revenue.

These aspects are all closely allied and require a great deal of forward planning, the guiding principles of which have been developed mainly on the Continent over the last half-century; upon these principles, good deer management in Britain can be based.

BIOLOGICAL AREA

The first principle to be established is that an area, inhabited by deer and representing their living space, must sustain the animals within its environment by allowing for the animals' health as well as providing adequate and balanced food and water. Remove any of these three requisites, or give them inadequate attention, and the condition of deer will deteriorate; sickness will occur sooner or later, and the deer will either move or die. Unfortunately, research on the relationship between the numbers of deer and the carrying capacity of the habitat in Britain is still in its infancy, and some years may pass before concrete results are available. Continental research, however, proves invaluable, especially when considering woodland deer, and provides us with the basis of further development. The Scottish hill, as a deer habitat, represents a completely different problem, about which only limited assumptions and deductions can be made.

Unfortunately, the relationship between deer numbers and the habitat capacity is a most important issue, and the problem of overall numbers must be solved before the question of quality. The simple reason for this is that the best possible stock is unlikely to propagate and maintain its quality if the numbers of deer are excessive for the food available.

It would be wrong, however, to assume that because the carrying capacity of any given piece of land is uncertain the problem is insoluble and we should do nothing.

The first consideration is that, as a result of man's influence upon nature, an environment has been created in which the adult deer's only enemy is man. In bygone days, deer herds were attacked by bear, wolf, lynx and eagle; the weaker, wounded, diseased, single and young deer were under constant attack by predators and numerical control and regulation was thus enforced. This control now can be enforced only by man; even the eagle exists in such inadequate numbers as not to have much effect.

The second consideration, when examining the biological area, is that of other animals which live in competition with the deer. At this stage it is enough to say that, once again, there is little proven guidance on the subject; even worse, what guidance there is does tend to be confusing.

Logic would suggest that deer, inhabiting areas also used by sheep and other domestic stock, would be in constant competition for food with these animals which browse and eat grass—especially those which, like sheep and cattle, tend to take sweet grass and other ground growth. In broad terms, one could assume that an equation could be struck between deer's and other animals' food requirements roughly in proportion to their weight. Thus a deer weighing say 120lb would require three times the food needed by a sheep weighing 40lb. Therefore, for every three sheep taken off the hill an addition of one deer could be assumed without altering the habitat. Furthermore, this ratio has been and is being used on several estates, both in this country and on the Continent, with apparent satisfaction.

On the other hand, the Nature Conservancy Deer Research station on the island of Rhum reports (Ref 19) that the removal of sheep from the island has resulted in no apparent change in the quality of deer. It could be that the numbers were such as not to make a vast difference (approximately 25,000 acres, 1,700 sheep and 50 head of cattle and 1,600–1,700 head of deer, on average, between 1957 and 1967). It could be said that, even without sheep and cattle, the density is too high, and to a degree the removal of domestic stock has made only a marginal difference. (Deer density of 1 deer to 14·7 acres, plus other animals, equated at 3 sheep = 1 deer, 1 head of cattle = 2 deer, would produce a density of 1 deer 'unit' to 10·55 acres, whereas the Red Deer Commission for Scotland suggests about 1 deer:24/29 acres as an average. Even at this level no vast improvement of quality so far seems possible.) It is clear, however, from experiments and practice in various parts of the world, that when deer numbers are rightly adjusted to the capacity of the area, vast improvement in quality can be expected; the Scottish red deer shipped to New Zealand stand witness to this.

CONSTITUTION OF THE HERD

Whilst the subject of the deer/area relationship may seem so far inconclusive, the question of the constitution of deer stock, in the sense of proportion of sexes, calving rates, etc is easier to clarify.

The principles upon which the evidence is based are as follows.

Firstly, nature provides a sex ratio of approximately one hind to one stag. The sexing of calves suggests that this proportion of 1 : 1 or thereabouts is natural, and in fact there are indications that because the mortality rate of very young male calves is marginally greater than that of female calves, more male calves may be born than females.

Secondly, where predators are still in control, they kill more hinds than stags; the stag can defend himself with his antlers and is not quite as restricted as a hind would be when either carrying or leading a calf.

Thirdly, the assumption that because a stag can cover a multitude of hinds during the rut he should be allowed to do so is misleading because, in the still-existing primeval forests influenced by predators (and therefore existing under natural conditions), a stag rules two to four hinds for a period of his rut, and this hind group may change their master three to four times over the rutting period. In this way a stag does not lose his condition to nearly the same degree as one which masters a large herd.

Finally, if a single stag dominates over a large group of hinds, he will be exhausted at the end of the rut; he enters the winter season in poor condition and is therefore prone to the effects of malnutrition, disease etc (a stag can lose over 20 per cent of his weight in the rut and thus starts the lean period of the year with inadequate reserves of fat). Roebuck are affected in a similar fashion. Normally, roe pair during the rut and, having spent the rut with a doe or two, the buck will rest. With a large number of does the buck is unable to rest and exhausts himself covering too many does. He is luckier than the red deer stag, however, in having several months in which to recover before winter; on the other hand, he has to build his antlers during the winter months. If the proposition that the optimum ratio of sexes of one to one is accepted, then attention has to be paid to the age structure of the deer inhabiting the area. To this end the Hoffman Pyramid (Appendix 3) is used. The distribution of ages is important, for it provides the landowner with an adequate proportion of breeding stock and allows for a proportion of good mature and older stags as the prime objective of stalking. The justification of sex and age distribution, and the adjustment of existing stock ratio to conform with the Hoffman principle, will be evident from the study of the pyramid.

It is comparatively easy to talk or write about, and conform to, age distribution of stock in relation to farm animals, where records of birth dates, weights, milking, disease, etc can be meticulously kept; where deer are concerned, more skill and effort are needed in establishing the structure of age and in culling the right sort of animal.

RED AND FALLOW DEER

If the given objective of a natural sex ratio and fair distribution of ages in the herd is accepted, then any significant deviation from a one to one ratio in favour of the hinds results in excessive annual increase of calves—at which point the control of numbers becomes difficult.

A herd of 120 deer, with the ratio of 1:1, would have 60 stags and 60 hinds. With an average annual calving of about 60 per cent,* 36 calves would be born. With a ratio of 1:2 (and therefore 40 stags and 80 hinds), the calving would produce a total of 48 calves. If the herd is to be contained at the level of 120 this would mean that with the ratio of 1:1, 36 beasts have to be shot; with the ratio of 1:2, 48 beasts, or just about 40 per cent of the herd, would have to be taken.

In an area where there is a high proportion of hinds, a disproportionately high number of hinds between the ages of three and eight (ie, the best breeding age) has to be culled. Furthermore, with this imbalance, only a few stags, if any, can survive to the age of full antler development, and clearly even fewer can live to an advanced age. Even if a high number of calves is taken every year, an incredibly accurate, age-based, selective shooting plan,

---

* A 60 per cent rate is accepted on the Continent, the counting being done soon after the dropping season. The Scottish figure of 35–45 per cent is taken at the spring count and thus excludes the calves which perish in the first eight months of their life, so accounting for the mortality during the first winter.

requiring much time, experience and patience would have to be operated to ensure success.

If we take the generally accepted Scottish figure, of calving rate and first winter survival, of some 40 per cent (spring count) the principles do not change. With the ratio at 1:1, 60 hinds will produce enough calves for 24 to survive to the spring; to maintain the level of 120 we must shoot 24 animals of age 1 year and over. We therefore have the 'take-out' rate of about 20 per cent. At the ratio of 1:2, 80 hinds will produce enough calves for 32 to survive till spring and therefore 32 animals would have to be shot during the subsequent season, or 27 per cent of the stock. In either case, therefore, the control problem increases with the increase in the proportion of female animals.

In an ideally constituted herd, the age distribution at the ratio 1:1 could be presented as follows.

Hinds over 3 years, in proportion to younger hinds: 4:1 or 3:1
Calving expectation: older hinds 75 per cent, younger hinds 40 per cent
Stags: Young, up to 6 years: 55 per cent
　　　Middle-aged, 7–10 years: 30 per cent
　　　Old, over 10 years: 15 per cent

This generalisation is good enough in broad terms, when planned management is first conceived. Once management has been established on a firmer footing, the Hoffman Pyramid principle, giving a detailed age distribution in one-year age bands, ought to be applied.

The Hoffman Pyramid represents the ideal age distribution in a herd of a given size. It assumes that the environment provides sustenance and conditions in which the stags can live to the age of fourteen (in the pyramid presented), and that the hinds over the age of twelve do not normally bear healthy calves.

Assuming that an area has a given capacity, our aim must be to ensure that the deer population is adjusted, by the end of the shooting season, to that capacity figure; if we use the spring count as the basis of our calculations, the addition of the current year's calves may be disregarded. However, this does not mean that we can allow ourselves to forego the shooting of a proportion of calves during the hind-shooting season.

The object of planned shooting is to adjust the distribution to the required numbers, ideally in each age bracket. It is obvious that if, owing to mismanagement, the distribution of the total number of either sex or both sexes has become out of hand, the adjustment may have to be carried out over a period of several years. For instance, if we have too many beasts, and none of them is over ten years old, it will take us at least four years to build up the stock to include fourteen-year-old animals.

The Hoffman Pyramid can be used for construction, from past records of each year's shooting, of the age distribution and size of the current stock, provided the animals taken each year have been carefully and accurately aged, that calf counting has been accurate and, of course, that the number of animals that died (or have been poached) can at least be approximately assessed. The pyramids in Appendix 3 are those for areas which can hold about 200 red deer and 100 roe deer.

The pyramid in Appendix 3 representing red deer is in fact a presentation of a period of ten years during which both the age distribution and the total population of deer have been adjusted from a ratio of about 1:1·5 to 1:1.

For the purpose of our planning and forecasting we have to accept that the optimal age grouping allows for a balanced distribution. This is important because, amongst the hinds, excessive numbers of young beasts will cut the calving rate, and among the

TABLE 17

PERCENTAGE DISTRIBUTION BY AGE (RED DEER)

Age	Stags	Hinds
Calves	14%	14%
1 year		
2 years	40%	25%
3 years		
4 years		
to	60%	75%
12 years and older		

stags, too high a number of young stags does not allow for presentation of suitable trophies to the sporting tenant.

Ideally the distribution to aim at should be more or less as shown in Table 17.

This distribution can, and should, also be presented by classification of animals by quality, as shown in Table 18.

TABLE 18

CLASSIFICATION IN FOUR QUALITY CATEGORIES
(RED DEER)

		Good quality beasts Group A	Poor quality beasts Group B
Young	Cat I	IA	IB
Mature	Cat II	IIA	IIB

We now have a variety of requirements to be met in a well-devised and well-executed shooting plan:

1 Elimination of poor quality beasts as the first essential, and elimination of old beasts beyond the acceptable age.
2 Maintenance of static size of the population, adjusted to the capacity of land, with correct ratio of sexes.
3 Achievement of correct number, and correct age structure, which calls for a cull of all age groups including calves.

To fulfil these requirements, the need for a means of ascertaining the ages at least within the band groupings and for recognition of the quality of the beasts before shooting, and subsequently a means of precise age estimation after shooting, must by now be evident.

By grouping our requirements in one table (Table 19) we can build up a complete quick guide to the shooting plan. Furthermore, we can use a similar layout to present the stock of animals on the ground. By inserting the actual figures in appropriate sections, showing the strength of animal population in each section, we can at a glance make a decision as to what may be shot during the season.

TABLE 19

COMPOSITE AGE DISTRIBUTION AND CLASSIFICATION TABLE (RED DEER)

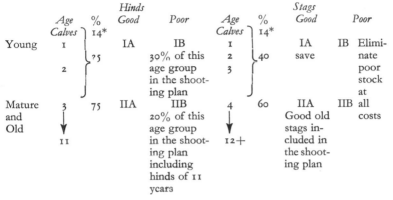

	Age Calves	%	*Hinds* Good	Poor	*Age Calves*	%	*Stags* Good	Poor
Young	1	14*	IA	IB 30% of this age group in the shooting plan	1	14*	IA save	IB Eliminate poor stock at
	2	?5			2 3	40		
Mature and Old	3 ↓ 11	75	IIA	IIB 20% of this age group in the shooting plan including hinds of 11 years	4 ↓ 12+	60	IIA Good old stags included in the shooting plan	IIB all costs

* It is important that in each sex calves represent about 14% of the total and that they are 'contained' in the suggested percentage level of 'young' animals.

ROE DEER

The broad principles upon which roe deer stock should be culled follow the same pattern as those applied to red deer, but allowances have to be made for the shorter life-span and earlier maturity of roe.

For the same reasons as those discussed in relation to red deer, the basic ratio of buck to does should be 1:1.

In broad terms, one can assume that in a given area the annual increase (with sex ratio of 1:1) stands at approximately 35 per cent of the total number of roe (assuming 70 per cent calving rate), which will increase to 53 per cent natural increase if the ratio reaches 1:3. Assuming, therefore, that we wish to increase the population, we can either reduce the annual cull or allow for an increase in the number of does in relation to the number of buck. The decision as to which method to adopt depends on the ability to enforce control ultimately, for once the desired number of animals is reached, the ratio of 1:1 will have to be restored. Of the two, reducing the annual cull is a safer method, even though it does mean a temporary reduction in the revenues derived from venison or stalking.

A point which is worth mentioning is that, on small areas with a low number of roe, a proportion of 1:1·5 may be found fairly easy to maintain, and indeed if the total population is at a level of about twenty animals the ratio of 1:1 may be a dangerous one as it will not allow for an adequate distribution of animals among the age groups. In fact, for purposes of effective management, roe holdings of fewer than thirty animals should be avoided if the normal principles of management are to be applied.

Here another point may need emphasis. When one talks of a deer-holding area, one is speaking of course of an area holding deer, and not of an estate or particular forest; a deer-holding area may therefore be either a part of one estate, or several estates with the deer population moving from one estate to another.

The broad principles for the calculation of roe stock plan, when it is desired to keep numbers static, should be as follows:

1 Total number of animals to be shot should equal the annual increase.
2 Buck of poor quality should be eliminated, ideally when they carry the first head.
3 Weak does, does with weak fawns, and indeed the weak fawns, must be shot.
4 Does aged seven years and over should be shot.

The analysis of the stock could be presented as in Table 20.

TABLE 20

HERD BREAKDOWN AND CULLING GUIDE (ROE DEER)

Age (years)	Percentage of the total	Sex ratios in age bands
Calves	25	Aim culling to sex ratio of 1:3 male to female
1	25	Aim culling to sex ratio of 3:1
2		
3		
4	20 max	Aim culling to sex ratio of 2:1
5		
6		
7	30	Aim culling to sex ratio of 1:2
8 & older		

Following the pattern of presentation of red and fallow deer, where all requirements are inserted into one table, we can produce Table 21.

TABLE 21

CLASSIFICATION IN FOUR QUALITY CATEGORIES WITH AGE DISTRIBUTION (ROE DEER)

| | | Does 50% of stock | | | Buck 50% of stock | |
	Age	good	poor	Age	good	poor
	Fawns			Fawns		Eliminate
Young	1			1		poor buck
	2	1A	1B	2	1A	1B at first
	3			3		head
				4		
Mature	4+	IIA	IIB	5+	IIA	IIB

These classifications can be transferred into the Hoffman Pyramid if required, as suggested in Appendix 3, Fig A2.

CHAPTER 9

CO-OPERATION

There can be nothing more frustrating for the owner or manager of a well-organised, predominantly stag, or hind, forest, than knowing or suspecting his neighbour to be taking unfair advantage of all the effort and planning, either by failing to shoot selectively or by not holding to the rules of culling.

Yet there are a number of deer forests which are basically single-sex forests, and where, as a result, a conclusive and well-designed management system on a single-sex forest basis cannot be established. The need arises, therefore, to discover or plot the migration movements, whatever their reason. Once the pattern is established, the basis for co-operation can be laid down. I do not suggest that only single-sex forests need co-operation between the owners, but these forests do need it more than mixed-sex forests.

The aim of the co-operation between two or more estates or forests is clear: to establish and maintain a suitable stock and shooting policy, aimed at relating the overall numbers to the feeding capacity of the ground and at establishing the required sex ratio between the hinds and stags, with suitable age structure.

This ratio and structure are important for several reasons already discussed. The main point is that one single-sex estate can ruin the efforts of the corresponding 'other-sex' estate through lack of interest or even through spite and greed.

The ideal co-operation between the forests or estates would be achieved through a process whereby they are formed into a unified block in which every service, function, obligation, benefit and privilege would be shared on the basis of proportions (for instance of area of 'deer acreage'), whilst all planning would be executed 'in committee' by the owners or their agents.

Page 151 (*above*)   Three good stags in velvet. (The rear left-hand stag is the 12-pointer development of the sideways-on fork shown in the top picture, page 133); (*below*) a collection of good fallow deer buck

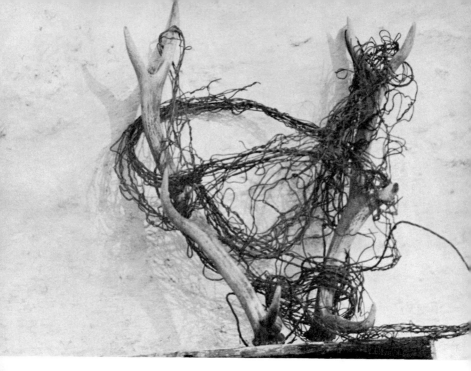

Page 152   Mishaps and mis-shapes. (*above*) The likely doom of deer living near soft wire mesh fences; (*below*) an interesting 'corkscrew' head

Such an exercise is not impossible but demands a fair amount of give and take in evolving a common approach to all matters both directly and indirectly affecting deer; this can have far-reaching consequences, perhaps of a financial nature, and especially in the early stages can be difficult and frustrating.

A sensible approach to such co-operation is that based on the observation of deer movements over a period of years, if need be, wherein the movements are of a regular nature. Consideration would be given to movements during the various seasons, taking into account food, shelter, mating habits, water, etc. There are often conflicting opinions concerning deer movements, whether they do or do not move from one area to another on a regular basis; in an exercise involving co-operation, the movement has to be studied by observation. It may be that, in a given situation, deer are 'self-sufficient' and are in fact static, in which case movement over the march may be sporadic and is not the *raison d'être* of creating a co-operative block of deer forests. From the information collected, however, such instances seem to be infrequent, on the mainland at least. Conversely, a closer study may reveal either that the movement is carried out over a wide area or that most of the movement is contained within only two or three forests or estates. Where one forest is predominantly hind-inhabited, for instance, the neighbour would normally be a stag area; the combination of these two can become a single management unit. This does not necessarily mean that there is no movement between this unit and its neighbours; nor is it necessary to combine only when one forest relies on the other, as is the case with hind and stag forests; all that is implied here is that between the stag and hind forest co-operation is obviously essential, whereas between mixed forests it is only advisable.

Where the life of one forest or estate depends on the other, the co-operation advocated can therefore be regarded in commercial terms as a vertical integration; horizontal integration would occur where the common policy is applied to similar forests or estate units.

The development of such co-operation, in either configuration, can be considered in a variety of ways with a variety of aims. The principal ones are:

Common shooting policy;
Common standards;
Common approach to feeding;
Common approach to utilisation of land;
Common economic aims and gains.

Each of these could be considered individually as an objective; several, or all, could be combined. The basic principles of each are elaborated below; all that needs to be discussed here is that, whichever field or combination of fields is adopted, each requires a total acceptance of mutually developed aims expressed in practical and comprehensible terms. The satisfaction of the co-operative need must therefore be the subject of discussion both in general terms and in detail; both have to be completely clear, understood and accepted not only by the owners but in all respects (particularly in practice) by the factors, agents, estate staff, shooting tenants or guests—for on their willing co-operation depends the success of the execution of such policies.

The five sections below describe the basic facets of co-operation under the appropriate headings, and are the essential requirements upon which further enlargement will be found elsewhere.

COMMON SHOOTING POLICY
The object here is to determine what philosophy, and what criteria of quantity and quality, should be adopted in shooting and culling. The details which have to be specified are not only in terms of what is to be taken off the ground—in overall numbers, ages, quality of animals, long and short term, etc—but also in the degree of expertise needed to accomplish the objective. Clearly, before such a policy can be adopted an understanding has to be reached on the number of deer the ground can, and should, hold.

Whilst it may be easy to ensure the execution of a given policy by the professional staff such as stalkers and keepers, guests and tenants may not be equally experienced, knowledgeable—or manageable; if they are not, to what sort of guidance, tests and control should they be exposed, in order to ensure that they conform to the objectives? Furthermore, how much authority should be given to the stalker so that he may make the decision, when taking out a guest or tenant, as to which animal may be shot?

It is imperative here to recognise that neither guest nor tenant nor stalker is infallible; that as the season draws to a close (often in very adverse weather during the hind-shooting season), the completion of the shooting quota may weigh heavily on the stalker's mind just as the long exposures to cold and wet influence his decision; should these considerations be accepted as important or not?

COMMON STANDARDS

The shooting policy, and especially its execution, will greatly depend on the common definition of the sort of animal to be shot. Every forest and every estate that regards its deer as an asset must have as its ambition the improvement of the species; increasing their body weight increases their value as venison; increasing their antler size, shape and quality increases their value as sporting trophies. In several recorded instances, consideration of body weight and antler improvement have developed ambitions so high that importation of animals from parks was resorted to in the attempt to improve the stock. One tends to forget in such instances that the prime influence on the quality of animals on the hill is the hill itself—what it can provide in terms of food, shelter, minerals, etc, all those ingredients which are indispensable to the well-being and development of the deer. It must be accepted, therefore, that the main and controlling factor in the quality of deer is the conditions under which the animals live. These conditions may be influenced; if the animals need shelter, woodland can be planted; if they lack minerals, these can be provided; if grass is sour, sweet hay can supplement the diet or good-quality grass growth can be encouraged. Basically, however, nature provides limits which impose the level of quality development beyond which animals cannot progress without human influence. This influence must be reasonable if it is to bear fruit; thus, transplanting deer from well-endowed parks to poor Scottish hill country may result in deterioration of the imported stock rather than the improvement of the existing herd.

When deciding on the standard, therefore, it is more important to establish what optimum criteria can be expected under the existing conditions than to seek to achieve the impossible or the unlikely. The initial standard to aim at without influencing or disturbing the living conditions is that of the top-quality animals already present on the ground. From such information, the subsequent standards can be developed.

COMMON APPROACH TO FEEDING

Feeding is, of course, closely connected with the local standard already discussed and with the land utilisation policy dealt with below. The most important facet of co-operation is that feeding should be uniform within the integrated area. This does not necessarily mean that exactly the same approach need be made for every part of the ground; for instance, if one forest lacks a mineral of sorts—say, calcium—there is no reason why this should not be provided and the results watched; such results may take the form of migration, improved body or antler development, etc. On the other hand, if, for instance, artificial feeding is introduced in an area subject to heavy winters, it should be carried out, as far as possible, over the whole of the integrated area of co-operating forests and be spread in relation to the density of animals so as not to cause migration of animals to food. Furthermore, it is important that feeding covers evenly the entire heavy-weather area; it is in fact better to provide small amounts spread evenly over a matter of several weeks during winter, than to dispense large quantities of food sporadically or locally.

COMMON APPROACH TO UTILISATION OF LAND

The question of land utilisation is an important one. In most instances, deer share the land with hill stock—predominantly sheep, sometimes cattle. From this fact two questions arise:

1 How many animals can the hill carry without the deterioration of feeding?
2 What are the economics, in practice and in theory, of mixing deer with farm stock?

Both the question of hill competition and that of deer economics are treated separately; at this stage, however, it is important to appreciate that, in the co-operative effort of the lairds, the necessity arises for the adoption of a common policy regarding the utilisation and improvements of land and feeding on the hill. Without such a common policy, the efforts of one estate can be spoilt by the non-co-operation of the neighbours. An important issue connected with land utilisation is that of marauding, an activity which is often related to overstocking and underfeeding. This does not mean that, if the hill is underpopulated by deer, the animals will not wander off the hill to feed on arable land—of course they will; deer are greedy—but obviously they will tend to raid crops to a greater extent when their habitat is poor in natural fodder and the competition for food on it is high than when the food is adequate and the field crops present no more than an added attraction or luxury.

COMMON ECONOMIC AIMS AND GAINS

It is a rare occurrence these days to find an estate that can be run regardless of economic considerations. In undertaking co-operation between estates, it is necessary to decide what assets and resources can be utilised by each estate of the co-operating block. Can a predominantly hind forest bring the same return per acre as a stag forest? Can each estate offer the same facilities during the stalking season?

Consider a block of three estates, one a stag forest, one a hind forest, and the third devoid of any deer during the stalking season but a favourite of hinds during the calving. The last gets no economic return from stalking, but is important to the survival of the deer in their physiological cycle. Must the third be the loser? Or can the other two estates risk not obtaining its co-operation?

All questions of this nature must be posed, and answered; often, where no easy answer exists, to provide a solution someone perhaps has to be generous in the short term in order that all can benefit in the long term.

PART THREE

DEER ECONOMICS

CHAPTER 10

ECONOMICS OF DEER—GENERAL CONSIDERATIONS

Unfortunately, the era in which estates were run for sport, amusement, hobby or pastime is over. Today, the landowner regards his estate as a collection of profit centres which must provide a return on capital invested; he must therefore consider deer as one of these profit centres.

Nevertheless, whilst industrial management, financial management and estate management have been studied deeply, game management is a comparatively new discipline, and the deer section of game management in the British Isles is virtually in its infancy. In the period of the last ten to fifteen years, however, much effort has been devoted to studying the problem of deer, which has been tackled from a variety of viewpoints and approaches, depending on the character of the sponsoring organisation. We have, therefore, a wide, but to a degree unco-ordinated and perhaps not always efficient spectrum of research having sometimes diverse objectives of viewing deer. The animals can be seen as part of the problem of conservation of the environment; as an ecological problem; as a range utilisation problem; as a farm animal; and as an economic asset. The diversity of views, approaches, opinions and working parameters is to a degree widened by the differences of habitat, from the Scottish hill to the densely afforested and agriculturally exploited, over populated areas, each incorporating different characteristics and widely diverging requirements.

From this situation four basic schools of thought have emerged:

1 Naturalists, to whom deer represent a part of the habitat which needs protection, facilities for study, etc;
2 Agriculturalists and silviculturalists to whom deer represent a danger;
3 Sportsmen who enjoy deer stalking;
4 Farm scientists who see deer as a potential source of protein.

Whilst these approaches are diverse, and often in opposition to one another, a feasible permutation can be worked out between them leading to possible clashes of interests but with only minimal risk of totally irreconcilable approaches or objectives. A situation exists, therefore, in which it is important to strike a balanced compromise allowing for satisfaction of most, if not all, interests; such a compromise can be presented as deer in the economics of the country or in the economy of the estate.

Much of the problem lies in the fact that all too frequently we fail to understand the behaviour of deer, especially the less common and more intangible of their characteristics.

An example of this, for instance, can be found in *The Field* of 3 March 1955, where a letter from Mary, Duchess of Westminster, drew attention to two points in the behaviour of deer: first, in winter, whilst looking for food, the deer will scrape through the snow and open the ground for sheep, while the herd of deer moving through the snow in single file makes a path along which sheep can reach lower ground; second, deer on the hill actually help to clean the ground of some parasitic infections—a suggestion based on veterinary research. Two such favourable arguments must carry some weight, even if in terms of economics they may be difficult to evaluate; it would have been easy to evaluate the loss of sheep stranded on the hillside and perished through lack of food or exposure.

There are other points which might prove of use as well as interest. Deer are browsers; in search of food in the ground growth, trees and bushes, they cover a fair area of ground and whilst browsing clear a great deal of undergrowth which could otherwise stifle the growth of trees. Admittedly this applies only to woodland deer; it is said that a pair of roe deer achieves as much clearing of unwanted growth in a year as a woodman working at it full time would do in two to three weeks, while red deer clear twice as much. Obviously the counter argument is that at the same time, they can equally do damage to useful growth; however, this point has been dealt with in Chapter 5.

An interesting aspect of deer economics was developed in a Russian journal a few years ago (*Pharmacopoeia*, date uncertain) which emphasises the utilisation of deer in the pharmaceutical industry. According to the *Pharmacopoeia* article, much research has been done in Tibet, Manchuria and China, inspired by the fact that deer antler formation is closely linked with, and related to, the sex gland activity; thus it was thought that antler and, indeed, other parts of the body might be of medical use and application, with results which, to a layman at least, seem quite staggering.

Proof of these claims is not available, but the article suggests that the Chinese and Tibetan researchers have explored the medical possibilities in fields as wide as invigoration of the human brain, strengthening of the bones and muscle, restoration of vitality in the body, treatment of gout, deafness, blood clotting, vaginal haemorrhages, sciatica, persistent coughs, asthma, pleurisy, and pneumonia. They have produced preparations from the antler — in the stage of development and as hard material—and from many parts of the body, including the mane and tail hair, for curing kidney disease, impotence, anaemia, and some spinal ailments; also the tendons and the stag's sex organs for the stimulation of human male sex activity and the treatment of impotence, and in complaints connected with menstruation.

This type of research into hitherto unexplored fields may well open new opportunities for economic as well as medical benefits; until now, however, such research seems to have been the prerogative of Russia, China and Tibet and little is known generally on this subject.

Setting aside such medical and economic considerations, however, the current emphasis on deer in the economy of an estate takes the form of:

1 Revenue from venison sold or consumed;
2 Revenue from letting of sporting rights;
3 Possible exploitation of byproducts such as antlers, skins, offal, etc.

All are valid and useful considerations, but all can be misleading.

Sporting value is difficult to estimate for at least two reasons: first, with a growing demand for leisure it is likely that the demand for stalking will increase and that this in turn will increase the value of stalking; second, the object of many a stalker is a good 'trophy', and these are not easily found in Scotland. If good-quality trophies were more plentiful, the revenue potential from stalking would increase. This is proved by the fact that the Forestry Commission obtains far greater revenue for a good stag from, for instance, Thetford Chase, than that obtainable from a Scottish estate, and the difference in price between the two works out in the range of 1,000 per cent. Furthermore, a large-trophy stag normally carries a large body and thus the venison revenue is also increased.

Whilst these are important and valid considerations, there is one other which may affect the economics of deer: 'by-products'. In many places the skin, liver, kidney, antlers, etc, unless wanted by the tenant or guest, are the recognised 'perks' of the keeper to whom they represent a value of several pounds sterling per year. Properly marketed, however, these by-products could represent considerable revenue to the estate: Europe is short of leather, all the more since in the last few years the clothing industry has made leather and suede fashionable; liver and kidneys can be manufactured into gourmet foodstuffs, antlers are sought for by button, knife and other manufacturers including ornament-makers; even hair could probably be used in the felt industry (especially since the demise of rabbit); guts and offal could provide pet-foods.

PRACTICAL APPROACH TO DEER AS AN ASSET

Appendices 5–8 are edited versions of papers that were presented by the author between 1970 and 1973 to a group of Scottish lairds;

in these papers two apparent aspects of management economics are discussed, whilst Appendix 4 provides some general points of guidance.

The aspects discussed in these appendices are stalking and the revenue derived from the sale of venison. The material available at the time of writing is inadequate to permit detailed assessment of the benefits to be derived from other by-products and their potential in the economics of the estate. This field is being urgently explored by sporting and industrial circles and we are bound to hear more on the subject in the future.

The question of placing a value on the trophy is discussed below (pp 170-9).

ROE DEER AS AN ASSET

This chapter has so far been concerned with the economics of red deer management, and to a degree with fallow deer. The problems of roe deer management differ in several ways. In the first place, roe deer, being smaller, represent a lower *per capita* value as venison (even if the connoisseur's demand for it may be high). Roe deer stalking is also a connoisseur's sport, being an art, whilst red deer stalking is more of a skill. An important consideration here is also the fact that roe deer are spreading in the British Isles and there can hardly be a place (except Wales) where roe could not be found within a forty or fifty mile radius. It is also not generally appreciated that many areas of Britain hold roe whose trophy value is of an international standard. Furthermore, the 'turnover' of roe, and their rate of growth and of coming to physical and sporting maturity, are faster than in the case of red deer. Finally, roe, coming into the shooting season in late spring, nicely fill a gap in the shooting calendar.

The second consideration is venison; a connoisseur of venison will take roe meat in preference to red deer, as being of a more delicate flavour and more tender. Revenue from roe, therefore, pound weight for pound sterling, should be considerably higher, and stalking rights on a capitation basis of £15–£20 per head of buck would be far from excessive, whilst the price of venison should be at least 50 per cent above that of red or fallow deer. On the other hand, the market, both for stalking and for venison, is at present still small, the selection is more difficult, and the danger to silviculture, especially in artificially planted young woodland, is greater with roe than red deer. For these reasons, the margins of profit which can be shown are likely to be narrow for as long as the market remains quiet.

CHAPTER II

ECONOMICS OF DEER—EVALUATION OF STALKING

Table 22 shows a forecast of changes which an estate of an 8,000-acre deer range could expect, if the policy of the estate was to be changed to conform to the variety of recommendations contained in this work. Certain items, however, require further explanation and some reservations have to be made.

ANIMAL WEIGHTS

It has already been stated that a stag loses weight during the rut, and that such a loss can be of the order of 20 per cent. It would be futile if, in the execution of the economic plan, all stags were to be shot before the rut in order to boost the return from venison, or after the rut, to prove that the plan was wrong in the first place. The essence of good management in terms of ecology is that selective shooting must be spread throughout the shooting season because:

1 A very good stag, well past his prime and therefore to be shot, should not be shot before the rut, for he is still a potential father of a first-class stag or first-class hind. He should not be taken until well into the rut, when he has been with his hind herd for a week or so; if the venison is not to have the typical 'rut smell' then he should be left until the end of the season, even at the cost of a lost proportion of venison revenue.

2 It should be possible, throughout the season, to shoot an undesirable stag, which either may have been elusive until then or may have appeared from elsewhere.

It could be said, therefore, that whilst as many stags as possible should be shot before the rut, a margin should be retained as a reserve; the size of this reserve is difficult to determine, for it must be related to the overall number of beasts on the ground, their general condition and other similar factors. Once a situation is reached when, by selective shooting, most of the real rubbish has been taken out, the rut and post-rut shooting reserve could be as low as 10 per cent.

The question of hind and calf shooting is different.

REVENUE F

(with stock adj

Year no	Count	Number shot	Hinds % sporting let possible	Venison sale average weight		Sporting rent
1	200	33	10	85lb	490	15
2	200	50			638	25
3	183	45		90lb	609	20
4	168	45			609	20
5	150	40		90lb	540	20
6	140	40	15		540	30
7	115	35			472	25
8	110	25	20	100lb	375	25
9	100	20			300	20
10	100	20			300	20

All current values and prices (venison @ 15p per lb, stalking as indicated).
Deer range: 8,000 acres   Deer population: 200 hinds, 100 stag
Deer density: 1:26·6 acres   Natural increase: approx 40% (spring
Aimed density: 1:40 acres

Selective hind shooting is difficult and it is important therefore to approach it with care. A hind's weight reacts to change of diet between the summer and winter, but this is a minor consideration: of greater importance is the practical consideration of winter stalking.

Because selection is difficult, one ought to give the stalkers as much time and as good weather as possible so that the greatest care can be exercised. For this reason, the earlier hind shooting is started (and finished) the better. There are two side benefits:

TALKING

ess)

Number shot	% sporting let (value)	Stags Venison sale average weight		Sporting rent			Revenue received	Total receipts
15	100	170lb	379	×25	375		754	1,259
15			379	×25	375		754	1,417
15		175lb	392	×25	375		767	1,396
15			392	5×25 \ 5×30 } 5×40 /	125 \ 150 } 200 /	475	867	1,496
15		180lb	405	5×30 \ 10×40 /	150 \ 400 /	550	955	1,515
15			405	5×30 \ 5×40 } 5×45 /	150 \ 200 } 225 /	575	980	1,550
15		185lb	417	5×40 \ 5×45 } 5×50 /	200 \ 225 } 250 /	675	1,092	1,589
15			417	5×40 \ 5×50 } 5×55 /	200 \ 250 } 275 /	725	1,142	1,542
15		190lb	430	5×40 \ 5×50 } 5×60 /	200 \ 250 } 300 /	750	1,180	1,500
15			430	5×40 \ 5×55 } 5×70 /	200 \ 275 } 350 /	825	1,255	1,575

To reduce population to 200 (33% cut).
To improve sex ratio to near parity.
To improve venison production   5% in 5 years
on pro rata basis   10% in 10 years.
To improve letting value of stag stalking to 200% in 10 years, 100% in 5 years.

first, the marginal loss of weight is smaller in early winter than at the height of it, and second, as calves are shot during the hind shooting season, the younger they are, the easier it is to spot their strengths and weaknesses. Once a calf is over six months old its size is well advanced and the differences between a well-developed calf and a weak calf can be difficult to spot. The difficulty diminishes at the end of winter when a poor calf would normally be very weak and underfed; by this time, however, the shooting season would have ended.

ANTLER EVALUATION

Table 22 shows a sample fluctuation of rent for stag shooting. One is frequently unsure how to assess the values, and how to charge for stalking.

There are two approaches to this problem, and neither is completely satisfactory. The method used more and more on the Continent, and in some British circles too, is to 'pay for what you shoot'. This method could be presented simply in tabular form as follows:

Basic fee: say, £25 (for shootable, selective, unwanted stags of nine points or under)
Additional fees:
Ten or eleven pointer £10
Royal £20
plus £10 per point for every point above twelve; thus a sixteen-pointer would cost £85 (basic £25 + Royal £20 + four extra points above twelve @ £10 each).

This method places the onus on the tenant to decide whether he wants to pay the fee for the particular beast at the time of stalking; on the other hand it could mean that a tenant establishes a right to 'bag' a good head if he is prepared to pay, regardless of selectivity as being a major consideration from the management viewpoint.

The second method is to establish a 'general value' for the forest; thus a forest where a well-established selective shooting

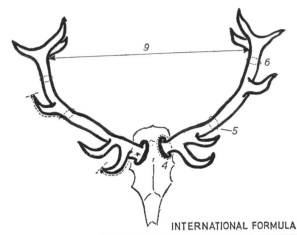

INTERNATIONAL FORMULA

			MEASURE	TOTAL	MEAN AV.	X-FACTOR	POINTS
1	Antler length	r / l				0.5	
2	Brow length	r / l				0·25	
3	Trey length	r / l				0·25	
4	Burrs circumference	r / l				1·0	
5	Circumference lower beam	r / l				1·0	
6	Circumference upper beam	r / l				1·0	
7	Number of tines	r / l				1·0	
8	Weight		$Kg \,^+_-$ grm. grm.				
9	Spread		$\dfrac{cm. \times 100}{average\ length\ cm} = \%$		Max. pts. 3		
10	Crowns				Max. pts. 10		
11	Bey tines				Max pts. 2		
12	Colour				Max. pts. 2		
13	Pearling				Max pts. 2		
14	Tine ends				Max pts 2		
	Total for 1–14						
15	Deductions				Max. pts. 3		
	TOTAL POINTS						

BRITISH MEASUREMENTS

Tines	r / l	
Length	r / l	
Beam	r / l	
Inside span		

19   Red deer antler measurement card—for CIC evaluation

plan has been successfully operated for some time, and good heads are therefore predominant, can charge a higher fee, because the chances of a good head are increased. One could say therefore that if one was taking a 'fifteen-stag forest' one could expect a greater number of good mature stags of high antler quality than in a ten-stag forest, and charge accordingly.

The evaluation of the antler values or qualities could be very sophisticated, based on CIC (Conseil International de la Chasse) formula with point-scoring by their methods (see Figs 19, 20 and 21) or it could be a simpler method, based on the well-established British practice, which considers the number of tines, length, circumference of the beam, span, etc.

Whichever method is adopted, it could be applied only to mature beasts, for instance red deer from the fifth head onwards, as being indicative of the general value of the forest.

Of course the value of stalking would have to be adjusted to reflect the 'market demand'; judging by the levels of charges in the Hungarian, Yugoslavian or even Austrian forests, where the price of a first-class head is, by British standards, exorbitant (although the standard of heads warrants it), topping £1,000 per head, there is much room for such upward adjustment.

Conversely, some charges by the Forestry Commission, for instance, in those forests where good trophies are to be found, are far in excess of charges in an average Scottish forest especially in areas where good heads are unlikely to be found. An important factor which must be remembered is that just as prices of a given commodity on the market change not only with time but also with the standard of the commodity, so the value of stalking can differ. A side issue which must also be taken into account is the ease of reaching the stalking ground, both from the point of view of its distance and ease of travel from the centres of population and also the ease of reaching the stalking ground from the local accommodation and therefore as affecting 'stalking time per day'; eg, if one can reach the stalking area within ten minutes of leaving one has a greater stalking-time potential than if one has to walk one hour to, and one hour from, the stalking ground; this

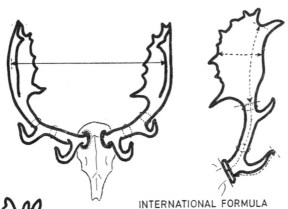

INTERNATIONAL FORMULA

	MEASUREMENT OF		VALUE	TOTAL	MEAN AV.	X-FACTOR	POINTS
1	Antler length	r / l				0.5	
2	Brow length	r / l				0.25	
3	Palmation length	r / l				1.0	
4	Palmation width	r / l				1.5	
5	Burrs circumference	r / l				1.0	
6	Circumference of lower beam	r / l				1.0	
7	Circumference of upper beam	r / l				1.0	
8	Weight			±		2.0	
9	Tines			Max. 6			
10	Colour			Max. 2			
11	Comparative valuation			Max. 5			
	TOTAL SERIAL 1 - 11						
12	Deductions			Max. 10			
13	Additions						
	TOTAL SCORE						

BRITISH MEASUREMENTS

Length	r / l	
Beam (lower)	r / l	
Palmat- ion width	r / l	
Tines	r / l	
Inside span		

20 Fallow deer antler measurement card—for CIC evaluation

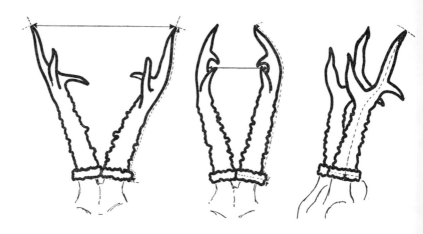

BRITISH MEASUREMENTS

Length Right_____ Left _____	Tip to tip _____ ins.
Circumference of coronet R. ___ L ___	Total number of points

INTERNATIONAL FORMULA

			MEASUREMENT	TOTAL	MEAN AV.	X-FACTOR	POINTS
1	Antler length	r / l				0·5	
2	Weight		grm	addition _____ grm / deduction		0·1	
3	Volume		ccm			0·3	
4	Spread		cm x 100 / (length average) cm = %			Max.pts. 4	
5	Colour					Max.pts. 4	
6	Pearling					Max.pts 4	
7	Burrs					Max. pts 4	
8	Tine ends					Max.pts 2	
TOTAL FOR SERIAL 1−8							
9	Additions (for appearance)					Max.pts 5	
10	Deductions (for appearance)					Max.pts 5	
TOTAL SCORE							

21   Roe deer antler measurement card—for CIC evaluation

recognises the paying guest's time-utilisation factor, though not necessarily his expenditure of physical effort.

The summary of the main location factors which may influence the value of stalking and the suggested weighting of these could be presented as follows:

1 Overall number of animals to be shot. The probability of a number of good heads obtainable in a large number of animals shot must be greater than if only a small number is available for shooting.
Factors: up to 5 heads = 0·8; 5–10 heads = 1·0; 11 heads and more = 1·2.

2 Ease of access to stalking ground. The less ineffective walking is needed, the higher percentage of time is available for stalking. Factors: 50% time effective = 0·8; 51%–70% = 0·9; 71%–85% = 1·0; over 86% = 1·2.

(The factors mentioned are only a suggestion and to my knowledge have not at the time of writing been applied; they can be changed to meet specific requirements.)

As the CIC formula is very complex, a quick estimation of antler quality using it is virtually impossible. It may be more appropriate, not to say easier, to use the British method, which places the main value upon the number of tines, the length, and the thickness of the beam and span (plus the width of palmation in fallow deer), and then applies a value conversion factor. A suggested set of values is shown in Table 23.

Having scored the heads, the price can be worked out according to the point totals as follows:

Red deer   £1·50 per point
Fallow deer   £1·00 per point
Roe deer   £0·50 per point

and then the locality factor can be applied to the value (as suggested previously).

Finally, recognition should be given to the general value of heads; it would not be fair to expect a high rent for low value heads. To this end, one could evaluate the general excellence of the area as related to average heads taken from the ground and award 'penalty factors' to the final price as shown in Table 24.

TABLE 23
METHOD OF ANTLER MEASUREMENT

Red deer   *Multiplied by*

Tines	Left	.... inches	1·0	=
	Right	.... inches	1·0	=
Length	Left	.... inches	0·25	=
	Right	.... inches	0·25	=
Circumference		.... inches	1·0	=
		.... inches	1·0	=
Inside span		.... inches	0·50	=

Total

Fallow deer

Length	Left	.... inches	0·25	=
	Right	.... inches	0·25	=
Circumference	Left	.... inches	1·0	=
	Right	.... inches	1·0	=
Palm width	Left	.... inches	1·0	=
	Right	.... inches	1·0	=
Tines	Left	.... inches	0·25	=
	Right	.... inches	0·25	=
Span		.... inches	0·50	=

Total

Roe deer

Length	Left	.... inches	1·0	=
	Right	.... inches	1·0	=
Tip-to-tip		.... inches	1·0	=
No of points	Left	.... inches	0·5	=
	Right	.... inches	0·5	=
Circumference	Left	.... inches	0·5	=
of coronets	Right	.... inches	0·5	=

Total

TABLE 24

ANTLER VALUE FACTORS RELATED TO SPECIES AND LOCATION

	Red deer	Fallow deer	Roe deer	Factor
Poor area	Good 10 pointer and better heads unlikely	27in heads unlikely	8½in 6 pointers unlikely	0·75
Fair area	10 pointer and better heads possible	27in well-palmated heads possible	9in 6 pointers possible	0·90
Good area	12 pointers possible, 10 pointers likely	27in well-palmated heads likely	9in 6 pointers likely	1·0
Very good area	10 and 12 pointers likely	30in well-palmated heads likely	Heads over 9in 6 pointers likely	1·05

We can now consolidate all the various points in an example
(Table 25).

TABLE 25

EVALUATION OF ANTLER POINT SCORE

Red deer

Points score (p 176)	$50\frac{5}{8}$ @ 1·50	=	75·97
but taken in a 5-stag forest	75·97×0·8	=	60·77
Access points, 75% time-effective	£60·77×1	=	60·77
taken in a fair area	£60·77×0·90	= £54·69

Fallow deer

Points score (p 176)	41·50 @ £1·00	=	41·50
taken in a 12-buck forest	41·50×1·2	=	49·80
Access 60% time-effective	49·80×0·9	=	44·82
taken in a poor area	44·82×0·75	= £33·61

Roe deer

Points score (p 176)	38 @ £0·50	=	19·00
taken in a 14-buck area	19·00×1·2	=	22·80
Access 75% time-effective	22·80×1	=	22·80
taken in a good area	22·80×0·95	= £21·66

One could continue to develop other factors not directly connected with stalking, such as the beauty of the area, domestic facilities offered, transport, travel and other facilities available, difficulties of stalking terrain, etc. Another important factor could be that, if it is the keeper's responsibility to decide which animal may or may not be shot, this will limit the ability of the tenant to take what heads he desires, regardless of the associated cost.

DEVELOPMENT POTENTIAL

An important element in the consideration of deer economics must be the development potential of the hill deer which, it has been suggested, is smaller than the potential of continental deer.

Arman (quoted in Ref 17) describes a research programme carried out at the Rowett Institute, Aberdeen. Two male calves were brought from the hill, both of three-year-old hinds originated from Rhum; at birth, their weights were 17½lb and 15½lb (8 and 7·05kg). One of the calves died at the age of one month of accidental injuries; the remaining calf was allowed to suck throughout lactation and had access to unlimited additional feed of dried grass and concentrates. He reached the weight of 147lb (67kg) at 5½ months and 165lb (75kg) at 7 months and by this age had 12½in (30cm) six point antlers.

Twelve additional calves were brought in at the age of a few days and were hand-reared on cow's milk; they were weaned at 7½ weeks on experimental food consisting of 85 per cent barley and 13 per cent fish meal, plus mineral and vitamin supplements. At the time of weaning they were divided into two groups, group 1 fed to appetite, group 2 to 70 per cent of the quantity of group 1. At seven months, a group 1 male reached the weight of 137lb (63kg), a female 110lb (50kg); at 8 months the male carried a 12½in (30cm) six-point antler.

Group 2 animals by the time they were 7 months old reached 88–99lb (40–50kg) males, and 84–88lb (38–40kg) females, but the males did not show any antler growth.

It is not intended to suggest that wild deer should or could be treated in the same way, but the experiment (which is continuing at the time of writing) does suggest that there is an enormous development potential in hill deer if they are well fed; that the rate of development depends on the food intake in terms of quality and quantity; and that feeding does result not only in body but also in antler development.

CHAPTER 12

DEER ECONOMICS—DEER AS ECONOMIC PRODUCT

So far, the expenditure side of deer management has not been considered, nor has the important point of the depth of financial involvement necessary if deer management is going to be regarded as an economically viable proposition.

Before becoming involved, however, one must accept the limitation of such discussion in abstract terms, for a great deal must of necessity be related to the given area. If an area of 100 units of land is to be fenced, for instance, it will require 35 units of fencing if it is circular, 40 units if square; if it is narrow and rectangular, it will require very much more—an area 100 units long and 1 unit wide will require 202 units of fencing.

As another example, 10,000 acres of low open hill can be overseen by one keeper, whereas 10,000 acres of high hill covered with dense forest may need two; in either case, if the keeper is also a shepherd he cannot cope with 10,000 acres of sheep, game and deer, just as one woodman cannot cope with 10,000 acres of woodland and game. On the other hand, a shepherd or a woodman can be of considerable help to the keeper if properly consulted, trained and motivated, without any disruption to his primary job.

One must therefore talk in generalities, in terms of principles rather than of detail. Later in this chapter, an 'account' is presented which might help to summarise the question of economic management; but before discussing the general principles of economic management, one must establish its aims, and subsequently elaborate on these as being the basis of action.

The aims of economic management should allow for the following:

1 The productive output, in terms of either venison or sport (or both) as the main objective;
2 The extent to which deer have to share the range with other interests—domestic animals, game birds, forestry interests, farming interests;
3 Co-operative effort with the neighbouring forests (if under different ownership or management).
4 Intentions and policies regarding animal improvement.

These considerations are of great importance and can be analysed briefly as follows:

1 If the estate is to be orientated solely towards the production of venison, the sex and age structure has to be established with that end in mind; a high proportion of hinds to stags can be accepted (5:1 would not be excessive), to ensure a high regeneration potential. Both stags and hinds must be healthy, with a concentration of age grouping probably of about 5–8 years in both sexes, for this is the age at which the venison yield is high, and fertility is high in both sexes. With this aim in view, calves are not shot unless obviously small and ailing, and old animals are completely superfluous. This policy is as near to 'hill deer farming' as one can get. Any feeding would be directed towards:

(i) Strengthening of calves by providing feeding places constructed so as to prevent older animals' access.

(ii) All animals to be fed for the purpose of body building, the food being given only a minimum of additives such as phosphorus, calcium, etc (which are mainly for bone and antler building).

(iii) Acceptance of the otherwise undesirable problem of a stag serving a very large number of hinds and spending himself during the rut, and a possible drop in calving rate which may result from a very high hind/stag ratio. Possibility of creation of shelters to help all animals, calves and stags in particular to cope with winter.

2 Range sharing by deer is important from the point of view

of feeding capacity (already discussed). There could also be a conflict of interests here. Dr J. D. Lockie (Ref 17) provides us with the figures (with additional notes by the Author) shown in Table 26.

TABLE 26

REVENUE OBTAINABLE FROM DEER

Nature of use	Sex ratio	Charges	Gross revenue per 1,000 animals		Author's annotation: revenue at current prices
1 Stag stalking	1:1	£50 per stag	£2,750		£1,375
Venison sale		10p per lb	£2,076		£3,633
			£4,826		£5,008
2 Stag stalking	1:1	£50 per stag	£2,750		£1,375
Hind stalking		£25 per hind or young stag	£2,050	(½ at	£410
Venison sale		10p per lb	£2,076	£10)	£3,633
			£6,876		£5,418
3 Venison production only	1:5	10p per lb	£3,496		£6,078
4 Hill sheep		Meat, wool and rate of breeding	approx £4,000		

Note Please see Appendix 9 for details.

Conversely, the sharing of the range with game, birds and animals can be fairly productive. In the first place, it allows the keepers to use their time most effectively, covering feather and ground game, and therefore not dissipating the human resources employed. The second consideration is the impact of deer on forestry and agriculture, not only in terms of costs attributable to damage, but also the higher feeding potential of woodland (therefore lower expense of feeding), shared cost of keepering (done by woodmen with game experience), natural cover during poor weather and the considerable influence of these upon the quality of deer, in terms both of weight and of antler. If the average weights of Scottish hill stags against woodland stags are compared, the weights would be some 14–15 stone for Scottish hill deer against 17–18 stone and more for woodland deer, and a general weight gain of 12–15 per cent would not be an exaggeration. Furthermore, in certain woodland and agricultural land inhabited by deer, weights of 25 stone (38 per cent gain) are not infrequent.

3 The degree of co-operation between estates is an important consideration, for the lack of it may force an estate with a good stock of deer, but with an unco-operative neighbour, to fence the area to prevent deer movements; such expenditure would clearly increase the overheads especially if, having fenced the deer, further expenditure had to be incurred such as provision of shelter, feeding improvements, etc.

4 If we regard deer as an investment, we must also consider what further input of capital can be accepted to 'service' this investment and to improve it in order to obtain a better return.

The following example gives the general concept of policy deliberations (with some details in Appendix 6).

The estate group used in the example, call it 'X', has a deer population of 1,589 head, culling 288 deer per year; of this number 33 are calves and the rest under ideal conditions would consist of 127 stags and 128 hinds of an average weight of 140lb and 78lb per head respectively. In value of venison this should produce £5,031, with a potential of £3,820 in stalking fees. An increase of 12 per cent in the quantity of venison would increase the return by £603. One could say therefore that against this possible gain the numbers could be reduced and allowance made for additional feeding, thus offsetting the costs against future gain. Such a policy would not only increase the revenue from venison but, if sensibly applied, would improve the quality of antler to an appreciable degree, thus allowing a considerable increase in revenue from sporting rights; if, for instance, we applied the figures quoted by Lockie to the value of deer stalking (£50), the revenue from our 127 stags would leap from £2,540 to £6,350 per year.

The policy statement for this group of estates could be formulated as follows:

1 To operate the deer forest with the primary aim of deer stalking.
2 To maintain the present land use policy whereby the level of hill sheep farming is maintained.

3 To develop the deer forest further for shooting, grouse being the main game bird.
4 To allow deer into wooded areas naturally regenerated, and into tree plantations over fifteen years old.
5 The estates comprising the group will co-operate in all matters, sharing costs and benefits on the basis of proportion of deer range acreage.
6 Because the deer range is primarily exploited for stalking, a pre-determined percentage (let us say 10 per cent) of the revenue will be re-invested for the purpose of deer improvement; to this end the following targets have been set:

> Numbers of deer to be adjusted to allow for a density of at least 35 acres per head of adult population (possible further adjustment to be considered at a later stage); sex ratio to be 1:1; natural feeding to be improved by establishment of feeding lawns and fields and fertilisation of existing grass areas; a proportion of re-investment will be for provision of woodland as shelter (long-term plan).

In discussing deer economics so far, reference has continually been made to red deer, and, more often than not, to considering Scottish conditions, the simple reason being that red deer are the most important species and Scotland the main area in the British Isles which holds deer. It is necessary, however, to consider the other species and other areas, in spite of the fact that little quantified and reliable information is available.

In a discussion of roe and fallow deer, there is the vexed problem of deer damage—owing to the fact that neither of these deer have adapted themselves to moorland living; furthermore, in discussing woodland, there is the added problem of those red deer that live in their natural habitat.

We have already discussed the density levels at which deer damage is cut to a minimum, without resorting to artificial preventative measures. The important factor in woodland deer economics is the acceptance of deer as a natural woodland dweller, and the exploitation of deer as a product, rather than their outright condemnation.

Assuming the woodland area of Britain to be—according to the official figures—in the region of 4½ million acres, the potential of woodland deer is enormous, but in this light one has to regard deer as a crop additional to—or to a degree replacing—the timber crop, over the period of timber maturity, of some sixty years.

If therefore a 10,000-acre woodland holds, for the sake of argument, 100 red deer and 50 roe deer—which by most standards would not be excessive—and the shooting is at the level of one-sixth of the red deer population and one-fifth of the roe, and if the sex ratio of both species is 1:1, one could arrive at the following:

1/6th of 100 red deer = 16 head per year, ideally 8 stags and 8 hinds to be culled. Weight of the woodland deer can be assumed as 200lb per stag and 120lb per hind.

1/5th of 50 roe deer = 10 head per year, ideally 5 buck and 5 does to be culled. Weights can be assumed as 50lb per buck and 35lb per doe.

Revenue potential:

Red deer

Venison;	8 × 200lb @ 17·5p per lb	£280
	8 × 120lb @ 17·5p per lb	£168
Stalking;	stags 8 @ £50	£400
	hinds 8 @ £10	£80

Roe Deer

Venison;	5 × 50lb @ 17·5p per lb	£43·50
	5 × 35lb @ 17·5p per lb	£30·50
Stalking;	Buck 5 @ £20	£100
	Does nil	—

Potential revenue, per year	£1,102·00
Potential revenue per 60 years of forest maturity	£66,120·00
or £6.61 per acre.	

The question now is whether deer do actually represent a loss to the woodland of the order of £6·61 per acre, especially considering that the vulnerable period in relation to damage is probably at the most the first twenty years, or one-third of the life span of industrial woodland; one has to remember also that a high proportion of the damaged growth would have perished anyway, deer usually being prone to damaging the weaker species.

Once the general concept of industrial forest management includes deer as a potential asset, the reafforestation planning can take deer into consideration and the various schemes already suggested can be incorporated and new schemes developed. Particularly attractive would be the scheme of wide rides (needed in any case for fire prevention) where an abundance of good-quality grass can be encouraged.

A variety of measures can be developed, aiming at concentration of deer in predetermined areas and at the same time providing facilities for the propagation of other game as an additional revenue potential.

It is difficult to provide a detailed analysis of the potential profit and cost of deer management in woodland, and the general principles which should be used have already been outlined. There is, however, a need to highlight the potential which deer stalking holds.

It is a fact that, with the rapid developments and improvements in the standard of living and the related search for leisure, game shooting and deer stalking are still under-exploited. When a comparison is made between the standards and prices obtainable on the Continent for really good stalking and those in the British Isles, it is evident that in the 'trophy-minded' countries charges for first-class trophies are several times higher than in Britain. G. K. Whitehead (Ref 20) states that at the 1971 International Exhibition in Budapest, of the twenty-two British roe deer heads exhibited, twenty-one were of Gold Medal class; had the best British heads been shot in Hungary, the stalker would have had to pay £960 for each of them. Likewise, in Hungary an average 'Gold Medal' red deer stag costs over £1,000, whereas in Britain the highest prices for exceptional specimens of roe deer are unlikely to exceed £50 and for red deer £200, while at average prices a red deer is unlikely to cost more than £30–£50.

There is no doubt that, for better heads, obtainable through better management and long-term planning, our prices could be considerably increased to provide an inviting return to offset any losses and to recompense the effort and the capital invested.

APPENDICES

CHEMICAL DETERRENTS

Developments in chemical technology in the last twenty-five years have to a great extent helped to combat deer damage, in two ways; first, by producing chemical feeding matter as an additive to natural food, and second, by the production of chemical compounds which, by their smell or taste (or both), deter deer from approaching individual plants or areas treated with them.

Since World War II considerable advances in this field have been made, particularly in Germany, Denmark and more recently in Austria, and in Britain some attempts have been made to manufacture suitable compounds for use in the fields and woodlands. Whilst our own chemicals have not been widely used, the continental ones have been, are being imported in slowly increasing quantities, and are being experimented with here on an increasing scale.

The reservations which one has to make in the case of chemical deterrents are those based on their limitations, drawbacks or even dangers. There are several basic requisites which must be adhered to: deterrents must be harmless to the growth of the plant which is protected and to that of plant life generally in the environment; they must not harm the fauna, and indeed must not be dangerous to humans; they must be easy to apply, cheap, durable and should not contain ingredients which discolour—even though one manufacturer has claimed that colouring of conifers through application of deer deterrents has considerably reduced Christmas-tree thefts during the Christmas period!

In most instances, application of deterrents is by spraying or painting and the speed of application obviously varies according to the properties of the materials used.

The list of deterrents that follows provides a fairly wide selection; it is important, however, to ascertain from the manufacturer or selling agents that the chemical to be purchased does not contain or bear any of the above undesired characteristics.

In only one case (known to the author), has any degree of human reaction to a deterrent been recorded, that of the Diana spray some years ago; since which time considerable effort has been made to neutralise the noxious effects. The Diana spray produced an onset of dizziness lasting some twenty-four hours, but without any further effect. Although, as far as can be ascertained, none of the deterrents quoted has toxic effects of a lasting or dangerous nature, no responsibility for their use can be accepted.

Some chemicals in group 12 have a powerful colouring component.

DEER REPELLENTS—USAGE AND MANUFACTURERS

Column 5 is key to list of manufacturers and importers (below).

Applied on	Against	Medium	Name of repellent	
Spruces	Browsing	Spray	Arbinol	1
,,	,,	,,	Diana	11
,,	,,	,,	Monacol	12
,,	,,	Paint	Arbinol	2
,,	,,	,,	Cervacol	12
,,	,,	,,	FCH 60 or TF 5	12
Firs	,,	Spray	HT 1	2
,,	,,	,,	Diana	11
,,	,,	,,	Monacol	12
,,	,,	Paint	Argon	3
,,	,,	,,	Dendrocol	4
,,	,,	,,	Mibacol	5
,,	,,	,,	Cervacol	12
,,	,,	,,	Silvacol	12
,,	,,	Spray	Coniferol SO 3	6
,,	,,	Spray or paint	Runol	12
,,	,,	Mechanical repellent	Vistrafaser	8
,,	,,	,,	Glaswolle (Glasswool)	7
,,	,,	Paint	HT 2	2
Pines	,,	Spray	Arbinol	1
,,	,,	,,	Monacol	12
,,	,,	Paint	Arbinol	1
,,	,,	,,	FCH 60 or TF 5	12
,,	,,	,,	Silvacol	12
,,	,,	,,	Cervacol	12
,,	,,	Spray	HT 1	2

Applied on	*Against*	*Medium*	*Name of repellent*	
Pines	Browsing	Spray	Coniferol SO 3	6
,,	,,	,,	Diana	11
,,	,,	Spray or paint	Runol	12
Deciduous trees and Larches	,,	Spray	Arbinol	1
,,	,,	,,	Diana	11
,,	,,	,,	Monacol	12
,,	,,	Paint	Arbinol	1
,,	,,	Spray	HT 1	2
,,	,,	Paint	Argon	3
,,	,,	,,	Dendrocol	4
,,	,,	,,	Mibacol	5
,,	,,	,,	Cervacol	12
,,	,,	,,	FCH 60 or TF 5	12
,,	,,	Spray	Coniferol 2	6
,,	,,	,,	Coniferol SO 3	6
,,	,,	Paint	HT 2	2
,,	,,	Spray or paint	Runol	12
New Plants	Browsing	Dipping	HT 1 and HT 4a	2
,,	,,	,,	FCH 60 or TF 5	12
,,	,,	Spray	Coniferol SO 3	6
,,	,,	,,	Monacol	12
,,	,,	,,	Diana	11
Spruces not younger than 11 years	Stripping	,,	Sinoxyd F	9
,,	,,	,,	HT 3a	2
,,	,,	Paint	Spangol	10
,,	,,	,,	Supertol	1
,,	,,	,,	Sinoxyd F	9
,,	,,	,,	HT 3a	2
Pines 7–14 years and Larches 10–20 years	,,	,,	Spangol	10
,,	,,	,,	Supertol	1
,,	,,	,,	HT 3a	2
Deciduous trees 8–30 years	,,	,,	Spangol	10
,,	,,	,,	Supertol	1
,,	,,	,,	Sinoxyd F	9
,,	,,	,,	HT 3b	2
,,	,,	Spray or paint	Runol	12
All trees	Fraying	Mechanical-chemical	HT 6	2
,,	All damage	Paint	Fegol	12
Arable land and meadows	All damage	Chemical with various methods of application	Anthropin	2

Applied on Area deterrent	*Against* All damage	*Medium* Impregnated sacks, etc, hung 10in above the ground	*Name of repellent* Silvacol K	12

MANUFACTURERS AND IMPORTERS (column 5)

1 Stahler, Stade, Hanover
2 Dr Hildebrandt, 24 Goethe Str, Kassel
3 Voitlander, Kronach
4 Avenarius, Stuttgart
5 Barthel & Co, Regensburg
6 Schiwanek, Pinding
7 Glasfaser Gesellschaft, Langenhagen, Hanover

8 Glanzstoff G.m.b.H. Cologne, Merheim
9 Von Sachs, Lahn, Marburg
10 Spangenbergwerke, Eidelstedt, Hamburg
11 Diana, Skovtjaere, Orehoved, Denmark
12 Anglo-Austrian Magnesite Co Ltd Sunningdale, Berks

PERCENTAGE ANALYSIS OF FODDER AND PLANTS WITH WHICH DEER MAY COME INTO CONTACT IN THEIR HABITAT

Food	Dry matter	Fat	Digestible albumen	Energy value	Calcium (CaO)	Phosphorus (P₂O₅)
MOIST FODDER						
1 *Green*						
Field beans	15·0	0·8	1·6	7·0	0·39	0·11
Buckwheat	16·5	0·6	1·2	8·0	0·4	0·1
Peas:						
beginning of flower	16·0	0·5	2·0	6·5	0·35	0·15
with pods	25·5	0·6	1·5	7·5	0·3	0·13
Vetch:						
before flower	16·0	0·4	1·8	7·5	0·25	0·12
in flower	18·0	0·4	1·6	8·0	0·26	0·12
Grass/clover mixture	17·0	0·8	1·9	9·5	0·16	0·12
Corn and leguminous plant (mixed)	20·5	0·8	2·3	10·5	0·34	0·18
Potato stalks (July)	15·3	0·7	0·4	5·5	0·85	0·13
Cabbage-turnip	11·5	0·5	0·5	5·5	0·66	0·2
Lucerne:						
in flower	25·0	0·7	2·4	11·5	1·12	0·12
2nd crop	24·0	0·8	2·6	10·5	0·93	0·14
3rd crop	26·0	1·0	2·9	12·0	0·95	0·14
Maize, half-mature	17·0	0·6	0·5	9·5	0·13	0·08
Carrot tops	18·5	0·9	1·5	7·5	1·5	0·16
Red clover:						
young	14·5	0·5	2·0	8·5	0·35	0·08
before flower	17·5	0·6	1·9	10·0	0·52	0·09
flowering	23·5	0·8	1·9	12·0	0·74	0·11
late	31·0	0·8	1·8	13·0	0·9	0·11

Food	Dry matter	Fat	Digestible albumen	Energy value	Calcium (CaO)	Phosphorus (P₂O₅)
Beetroot leaves	11·5	0·4	1·3	6·5	0·16	0·08
Spring greens:						
early	14·0	0·6	1·6	6·8	0·43	0·21
flowering	18·0	0·7	1·7	8·5	0·42	0·22
Sweet lupin:						
yellow, in flower	12·0	0·3	1·1	7·0	0·17	0·07
young pods	14·0	0·3	1·3	7·0	0·16	0·09
running to seed	18·0	0·5	2·2	8·0	0·16	0·11
blue, young pods	16·0	0·4	1·5	9·5	0·6	0·9
running to seed	19·5	0·5	1·8	9·0	0·52	0·1
White clover	17·0	0·8	2·3	9·0	0·37	0·19
Grazing grass:						
early	20·5	0·9	2·1	13·5	0·25	0·19
in flower	22·0	0·7	1·7	13·0	0·27	0·24
Clover, mixed	18·0	0·6	0·6	8·0	0·57	0·1
Tufted vetch in flower	14·5	0·6	2·0	8·0	0·27	0·14
Sugar beet:						
leaves	16·5	0·4	1·5	8·0	0·17	0·1
tops	24·5	0·4	1·3	10·5	0·17	0·11
Beech leaves	20·0	0·0	3·5	8·0	0·35	0·1
Birch leaves	21·0	0·0	4·0	8·0	0·3	0·12
Oak leaves	20·0	0·0	2·0	8·4	0·4	0·1
Willow leaves	18·0	0·0	4·0	6·0	0·6	0·25
Willow shoots	15·0	0·0	2·5	4·5	0·5	0·2
Scotch pine needles	18·0	0·0	1·0	4·0	0·3	0·08
Spruce needles	20·0	0·0	0·8	3·5	0·2	0·1
Heather	25·0	0·0	1·8	5·0	0·13	0·06

2 Roots and bulbs

Fodder beet	11·0	0·4	0·5	7·0	0·04	0·08
Potato	25·0	0·1	1·0	19·0	0·03	0·15
Carrots	14·0	0·2	0·8	10·0	0·07	0·11
Sugar beet	24·5	0·1	0·5	16·0	0·06	0·08

3 Moist industrial by-products

Brewer's grain	20·5	1·5	3·2	11·0	0·15	0·39
Potato pulp	12·0	0·0	0·1	8·0	0·05	0·03
Rape cake	8·5	0·1	0·3	5·0	0·11	0·02

DRIED FODDER

1 Hay

Vetch, dried	84·0	2·3	11·0	30·5	1·65	0·6
Mountain hay	86·0	2·8	5·6	39·6	0·71	0·27
Mixed grass and clover	86·0	2·0	5·0	36·0	0·56	0·53
Dried potato stalks	86·0	2·9	3·0	29·5	3·15	0·22
Mixed dried leaves	80·0	0·0	8·0	33·0	1·6	0·4

Food	Dry matter	Fat	Digestible albumen	Energy value	Calcium (CaO)	Phosphorus (P$_2$O$_5$)
Lucerne hay:						
early cut	86·8	2·1	8·2	31·6	2·5	0·55
2nd crop	86·8	2·3	8·8	34·0	2·24	0·44
3rd crop	86·8	2·5	10·6	38·0	3·11	0·43
flowers	85·0	4·2	16·2	49·5	4·78	0·54
meal	92·0	2·0	8·8	29·0	2.75	0·8
stalks	85·0	2·3	3·2	21·5	1·28	0·3
Red clover:						
young	86·0	2·0	7·0	36·5	2·35	1·05
flowering	87·0	3·7	5·8	31·0	2·03	0·58
2nd flower	86·6	1·8	4·0	33·0	1·6	0·45
uprooted	84·5	2·8	6·0	27·0	2·52	0·73
uprooted (2nd crop)	86·0	2·0	7·2	32·5	2·0	0·38
meal	88·0	2·4	10·3	42·0	2·4	0·58
Sweet grass	86·0	2·5	4·0	30·5	0·67	0·72
Sweet lupin, in flower	86·0	1·5	9·0	33·5	0·93	0·61
White clover hay	85·5	3·5	5·4	32·5	1·85	0·76
Meadow hay:						
early	86·0	3·3	6·5	46·0	1·45	0·82
medium	87·5	3·9	4·1	36·0	0·95	0·65
normal cut	86·0	1·8	2·5	31·5	0·75	0·4
2nd crop	86·0	3·2	4·2	32·5	0·96	0·69
meal	86·5	2·4	9·3	40·0	1·21	0·7
Mixed clover hay	84·0	2·2	5·0	27·0	2·75	0·5
STRAWS, CHAFF, HUSKS						
Bean straw	84·0	1·3	3·2	23·0	1·59	0·29
Pea straw	86·5	1·6	3·5	18·5	2·23	0·23
Pea husks	86·0	1·2	4·0	20·0	3·15	0·44
Vetch straw	87·0	1·7	3·5	21·0	1·88	0·55
Lupin straw	84·0	1·5	1·6	19·5	1·7	0·21
Maize straw	86·0	1·3	1·0	18·5	0·43	0·19
Rape straw	84·0	1·2	0·7	15·5	2·0	0·25
Rape pods	84·0	1·5	1·0	12·0	3·51	0·37
Soya straw	86·0	2·0	3·0	1·6	1·46	0·31
ARTIFICIALLY DRIED FODDER						
Barm	90·5	1·4	41·5	65·0	0·3	3·23
Brewers' corn	91·0	7·5	14·0	51·0	0·44	1·37
Potato powder	88·5	0·3	1·0	58·0	4·14	0·29
Potato strips	89·0	0·3	3·0	75·0	0·05	0·55
Lucerne meal	92·0	1·8	1·1	36·5	2·65	0·75
Malt grain	87·5	3·3	13·0	49·0	0·19	1·82
Sugar beet cake	90·0	0·8	5·1	54·0	1·4	1·5

Food	Dry matter	Fat	Digestible albumen	Energy value	Calcium (CaO)	Phosphorus (P_2O_5)
ENERGY FODDER						
1 *Grain and fruit*						
Field beans	85·0	1·4	21·8	70·0	0·23	1·16
Bitter lupin:						
yellow	86·0	4·5	30·5	67·0	0·28	1·43
blue	86·0	6·0	23·0	71·0	0·25	1·4
white	86·0	7·0	23·0	72·0	0·25	1·41
Fresh acorns	50·0	2·4	2·2	40·0	0·1	1·15
Peas	85·0	1·4	17·5	69·5	0·11	0·88
Barley fodder	86·0	2·0	7·0	67·0	0·08	0·58
Vetch fodder	87·0	2·0	20·0	65·6	0·15	1·05
Oats	87·5	4·8	7·0	60·0	0·14	0·63
Chestnuts	50·8	1·5	1·5	34·0	0·2	0·00
Flax	91·0	34·5	19·5	120·0	0·32	1·37
Maize	87·0	4·2	7·2	80·0	0·05	0·75
Rye	86·0	1·5	8·3	73·5	0·06	0·8
Soya beans	91·0	16·0	33·0	78·0	0·26	1·68
Sweet lupin:						
yellow	91·0	4·3	34·0	65·6	0·35	1·03
blue	86·0	4·0	25·0	69·0	0·3	0·63
Wheat	87·0	1·8	9·2	71·5	0·13	0·73
2 *Industrial by-products*						
Fodder sugar	95·5	12·4	13·3	75·0	0·64	0·09
Barley fodder meal	87·0	3·0	9·0	74·0	0·18	0·64
Cornflour meal	89·5	10·2	23·0	71·0	0·5	2·97
Malt extract	87·5	3·6	5·7	65·0	0·04	2·73
Molasses	78·5	0·0	0·0	44·0	0·5	0·05
Rye flour extract	87·0	3·1	11·3	52·0	0·18	2·04
Oats flour extract	87·0	4·3	11·0	50·5	0·2	2·41
3 *Oil cakes*						
Ground nut cake	91·0	10·5	21·0	45·0	0·16	1·06
Linseed oil extract	89·0	6·5	29·6	70·6	0·43	1·65
Rye cake	90·0	7·7	27·0	59·0	0·72	1·92
Soya cake	89·0	5·5	39·5	75·0	0·51	1·5

THE MAIN FODDER RECOMMENDED FOR DEER DURING
THE WHOLE YEAR
(all values in per percentages)

	Dehydration	Nitro-free substance content	Digestible albumen	Calcium	Phosphorus
Lucerne, fresh	22·0	9·0	2·5	0·9	0·14
Red clover, fresh	20·0	8·0	2·0	0·7	0·1
Sweet lupin, fresh	15·0	6·0	1·8	0·17	0·07
Heather	25·0	4·0	1·8	0·13	0·06
Meadow grass	20·0	6·0	1·7	0·2	0·2
Lucerne hay meal	92·0	35·0	8·8	2·7	0·8
Oats extract	87·0	52·5	10·3	0·2	2·41
Rye extract	87·0	52·0	10·0	0·2	2·1
Sweet lupin seed	90·0	23·0	40·0	0·3	1·0
Soya bean	88·0	30·0	40·0	0·53	1·5
Chestnuts	50·0	45·0	1·5	0·2	0·0
Acorns	50·0	45·0	2·2	0·1	0·15
Potato	25·0	19·0	1·0	0·03	0·15
Fodder roots	11·0	7·0	0·5	0·04	0·08
Sugar beet	24·5	16·0	0·5	0·06	0·08
Lucerne hay	87·0	32·0	10·0	2·4	0·5
Red clover hay	87·0	33·0	7·0	2·0	0·6
Grass hay	86·0	30·0	6·5	1·0	0·6
Dried leaves	85·0	35·0	5·0	2·0	0·2

MAIN TYPES OF FODDER RECOMMENDED FOR WINTER
(JANUARY–JUNE)

	Quantity	Digestible albumen	Nitro-free contents	Calcium	Phosphorus
Lucerne meal or finely cut lucerne hay	1·1	0·11	0·37	0·026	0·006
Oats extract	2·0	0·23	1·2	0·014	0·052
Soya beans Ground nuts }	2·0	1·9	0·7	0·015	0·04
Potatoes	1·1	0·15	0·75	0·006	0·009
Lucerne or red clover hay	3·8	1·75	1·5	0·15	0·002

BRITISH MANUFACTURED COBS

	Protein %	Oil %	Nitrogen %	NaCl %	Phosphorus %
Hutchinson Stag Cobs	11·6	0·76	1·8	0·46	0·5
BOCM Hill Cow Cobs	15·0	1·45	2·5	1·70	0·6

THE HOFFMAN PYRAMID

Let us assume that on a given estate we have a number of deer; all we know about them is that there are 73 stags, 126 hinds and 44 calves.

We have made a decision to adjust the stock to a level of about 200 head total, with equal numbers of stags and hinds, giving ourselves ten years to achieve it. This means that we have to take more hinds than stags every year. Because we are unable to sex the calves we assume that the 44 calves are about half male and half female. By present-day evidence, we can take annually about one-sixth of the stock to retain the overall population size.

We accept that calves have to be shot, especially the weaker ones, and we decide to decrease the existing stock in the first year by 10 stags, 27 hinds and 8 calves (just more than one-sixth). It transpires that of the 8 calves 3 were female and 5 male, and we establish the ages of the adult animals shot (black squares, fig A1). Our activities are represented in the pyramid (above the thick black line with centrally placed ages C—15), (marked START).

Each year is approached in a similar manner.

The following year we count our beasts and find:

$73 + 16 - 10 = 79$ stags; $136 + 20 - 27 = 129$ hinds and 46 calves

Our calves are now shown below the 'START' line, and our shooting plan executed is shown (year 10). We follow the pattern year after year; by shooting a high proportion of hinds we may effect a drop in the number of calves; we extend the pyramid downwards, by adding each successive year's calves as a new line.

It may be said that the method allows for no natural mortality;

in fact it does. If we decide that the shooting plan allows for the first year to account for 10 stags, 27 hinds and 8 calves, two of each may have died of natural causes; and therefore the shooting of 8 stags, 25 hinds and 6 calves would be required. The figures representing the natural mortality can either be taken off, as an allowance from the shooting plan as expected to perish during the year, or allowance can be made for them (those found dead) in the subsequent season's shooting plan.

One could also suggest that the reconstruction of the composition of the herd was impossible unless one knew the exact composition of the herd by sex and age at the start; in fact this is not so. The situation below the 'START' line provides us with the solution. Provided our age estimation of the animals killed (or found dead) each year, and the count of calves each year, are accurate, and provided that in one way or another we have accounted for mortality, composition of the herd at ages below 10 years should be accurate.

Provided, therefore, our age recognition of the dead animals is correct, we can achieve our target of reducing the number of hinds and more or less retaining the overall number of beasts and reducing the hind-to-stag ratio, but this has to be planned and executed with care. The important requirement throughout this ten-year period, is to judge the ages and quality not only of the beasts when they are killed but also of those on the hill, and to plan the age distribution of the animals to be shot so as to retain the 'shape' of the pyramid.

We are now in a position to decide on the shooting plan for the next year. There is no 'copybook' answer to this question and only a suggestion can be made; one would imagine a quota divided as follows:

	c	1	2	3	4	5	6	7	8	9	10	11	12	13	14	15	
Hinds	3	2	1	1	2	–	1	1	1	1	1	1	2	1	–	1	= 19
Stags	2	1	1	1	1	1	2	1	1	1	1	–	–	–	1	1	= 15

STAGS

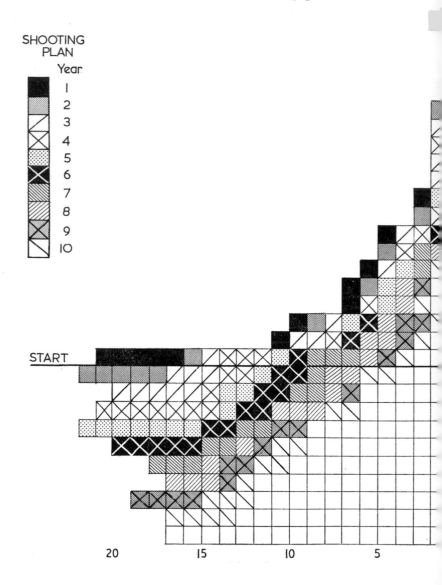

SHOOTING
PLAN
Year
1
2
3
4
5
6
7
8
9
10

START

20   15   10   5

HINDS

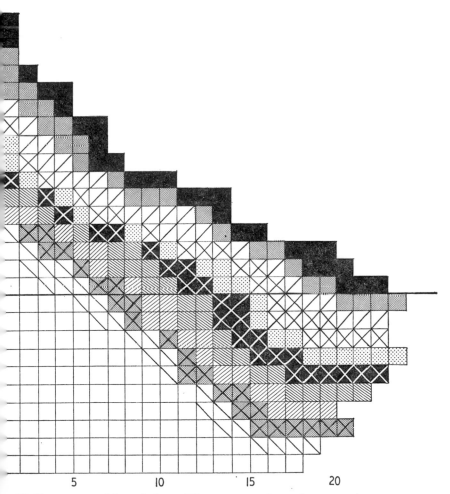

Hoffman pyramid, red deer. The presentation of consecutive
shooting plans in order to provide an idea of the age and sex structure
of the herds of an estate (or estate group)

Doe

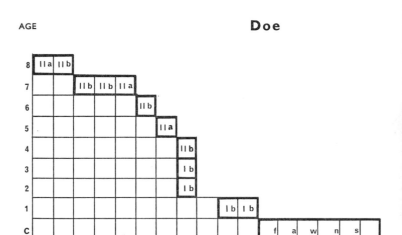

Buck

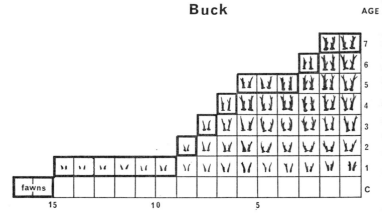

A2 Hoffman pyramid, roe deer. The presentation of the plan over one year with visual indication of the type of buck to be shot (or saved)

BASIC PLANNING OF DEER MANAGEMENT FOR ECONOMIC RETURN

Based on a lecture delivered by the author
to the West Highlands Branch of
the British Deer Society,
November 1972

The object of this presentation is to illustrate an approach to methodical deer management, showing the impact of age and sex structure upon the development and control of deer population and upon the economic considerations of deer management.

To most estates, deer represent either an economic asset, through revenues derived from deer stalking, disposal of venison or even wider utilisation of land, or the discharge of social obligation through preservation of species and conservation of environment and habitat. The discharge of the 'social obligation' in relation to the preservation and conservation of species is a *sine qua non*; the realisation of the economic potential is, to a large extent, a matter of management method and therefore within our power to influence. We shall discuss some ideas as to how both can be enhanced through planning.

Deer management has four basic concepts which have to be considered and solved as a matter of priority before success can be achieved:

1 Decision on the holding capacity of the ground
2 Sex ratio among the animals on the hill
3 Age structure among the beasts
4 Selective shooting, premise and practice.

Appendix 4

HOLDING CAPACITY

A decision has to be reached as to how many deer can be adequately sustained on a given area of land, allowing not for mere survival but for optimum development of the species in body and antler, as related to the natural environment. The potential capacity of land will of course depend upon the biological, geological and climatic conditions. Because all variables in this consideration are related to the location, detailed discussion is not possible in the abstract. It can be said only that there are some 180,000 red deer in Scotland with a density of about 17–39 acres per head, whereas the analysis of food requirements and food supply position, and the incidence of damage analyses, in many good-quality forests on the Continent and in Britain suggests a density of between 50 and 100 acres per head, or indeed even more, as providing optimal conditions for the realisation of development potential under natural conditions. I know that the deer density in Scotland is related to the forest area as presented on the map and not the actual ground surface in relief, but even if one were to work out the actual ground surface, the maximum change one would obtain would be about 30 per cent and therefore our 17–39 acres per head would, at the best, become 22–50 acres per head; thus we might reach the very bottom of the scale which applies to good-quality feeding areas, whereas Scotland must be accepted as being on the whole a poorish area in this respect.

SEX RATIO AND AGE STRUCTURE

The population structure of deer is largely dependent on the methods of management, which should have the following aims. In relation to stags:

1 To allow for elimination of poor-quality animals as early as possible, retaining healthy and good-quality stock only, for reproduction.
2 To allow for a cull of old beasts as sporting trophies of high value, after the antlers have passed the peak of development.

3 To ensure maximum potential body weight and therefore optimum return from venison.

In relation to hinds:

1 To ensure the right number of good mothering hinds.
2 To eliminate poor-quality stock before females become fertile.
3 To ensure maximum potential body weight in order to obtain optimum return from venison.

These characteristics can be presented graphically as in Fig A3.

In general, this composite graph suggests that the weight of stags and hinds increases rapidly in the first four years of their life; from the point of view of venison production, therefore, killing of animals, apart from the necessary culling to control numbers and purity of breeding, is ill-advised until the beasts reach the age of 4½–5 years.

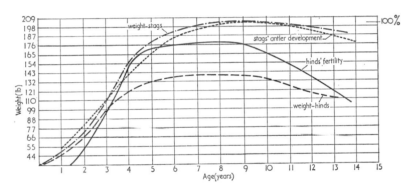

A3   Weight and development of stags and hinds related to age

Hinds' fertility and stags' antlers improve rapidly up to the age of five or six and thereafter one expects the antlers to develop further up to the age of nine or thereabouts; since fertility is over the peak by the age of nine, the cropping of both sexes should be planned in such a manner as to allow for the taking of as many animals as possible above that age. We shall be returning to this point a little later, when we discuss the age distribution of deer.

Appendix 4

Sex ratio and age structure have to be discussed jointly because they are related.

Sex ratio can be controlled effectively and comparatively easily by adjusting the annual cull to take a greater or smaller proportion of hinds in relation to stags. Of course, large changes cannot be effected and achieved in a short space of time, but, with structured policy and care in execution, much can be done in a space of five years.

In their natural environment, where deer are exposed to predators, the ratio of sexes stands at about 1:1. The assumption is, therefore, that this is the level which nature intends, and that this ratio has been upset by the human intrusion; we know that the development of deer under these natural conditions was better than it is today, hence the deduction that this ratio suits deer for their naturally good development.

The analysis of age structure starts from calves. If we analyse the calving rate, we find that it can be related either to the overall hind population or to the population of hinds aged three and above; it can be presented as:

either 80 per cent of hind population—aged three years and over
or   40 per cent of hind population across the age bands

Of course these figures will fluctuate somewhat between locations, but they should not change more than, say, 5 per cent especially if related to spring counts and therefore not requiring considerations of winter mortality.

Armed with these figures we can start planning.

SELECTIVE SHOOTING

Let us take an area of ground capable of sustaining a population of 225 head of deer. A deer's life span is about fifteen years. These two factors, life span and capacity of the ground, are our controlling factors.

We can present the population as a triangle (Fig A4). The height is the natural age span, and the base is the natural calf addition.

In our case the span of life is fifteen years and the capacity is 225; therefore the base must be 30 head of calves. This population can be presented as a base of 15 on the right and 15 on the left, as it is in the left-hand triangle, or let us say 20 on the left and 10 on the

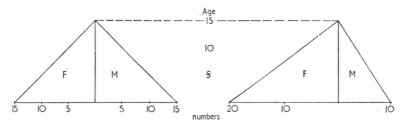

A4   Deer population presented as a triangle

right as in the right-hand triangle, representing female and male animals respectively, and therefore holding ratios of 1:1 and 1:2 male to female respectively.

Let us now take another area with a capacity of 300 deer.

At the initial stage of planning we may not know what the age structure of hinds is and we therefore have to use the figure of 40 per cent of hind population as depicting the calving rate; on this basis we shall arrive at the annual addition of 60 animals (40 per cent of 150 hinds). However, the shape of our triangle suggests that at this rate 60 calves represent a surplus of 20 calves over our capacity requirements, with the ratio of 1:1, and this surplus is shown as 10 male and 10 female calves respectively. As a result we have to eliminate the surplus calves to maintain the numbers (Fig A5).

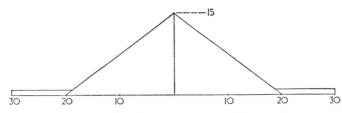

A5   Natural addition of calves presents us with a surplus

Many will ask, why eliminate calves? Why not let them live for a year or two and then cull them as adult animals and thereby increase the return from venison?

The simple answer is as follows:

1 An increase of young animals below calf-bearing age can be sustained (remembering the overall capacity of 300 animals on the land) only at the cost of older animals.

2 Whilst it is easy to recognise a calf among the older beasts, this ease decreases as the animal becomes 16–19 months old or older, and at the age of 2½ years it becomes difficult to draw the distinction. From the point of view of selective culling and especially control of numbers and ages, early-age shooting is therefore advantageous.

In any case, who wants to keep a weak calf in the byre?

If we were to keep the animals for three years to allow them to develop fully in the body, so as to optimise the return from venison, we should have a problem in having too many animals younger than three years old and not enough older animals to maintain the balance.

What I mean is that, if all calves were to survive and no young animals were to be culled, and we relied purely on natural mortality, then, in order to maintain the level of animal population, we should have to cut the number of older animals by the same number as the surplus of the younger ones; we should have to cut the numbers of high-fertility hinds and mature stags, and we should never reach a stage where a high number of fully developed beasts were available for proper shooting at the right age.

In fact the age distribution of animals is not as even and simple as in the triangles we have considered, especially if we carry out our culling methodically. The reason for this is spelled out in our aims quoted earlier: to allow for a cull of old, well-developed stags, past their prime, and to foster the hinds at the peak of their fertility.

In consequence we are looking for a means of sustaining a maximum number of stags at the age of 11 and above, and of hinds between the ages of 4 and 9. As a result of these needs, our triangle 'bulges' in the middle of the age scale in relation to hinds and is elongated at the top in relation to stags.

Having established the basic shape of our 'pyramid' we can now use it for planning and recording our shooting policy by marking the animals (ie, squares in the pyramid) which are planned to be shot, and those which have been shot as the plan is being executed; the simplest way is to put a line across the square depicting an animal to be shot and to colour the square when the animal has been shot. It stands to reason that, using this method over a period of years, adding the annual increase of calves to the bottom of the pyramid, we can present an accurate structure of our stock, provided that we not only mark the animals shot, but also make allowance for the animals that die each year through natural and other causes.

To be accurate, however, this approach requires us to be able to age the animals on the hoof both at the time of annual counting (to verify the pyramid) and at the time of shooting (to shoot only the selected animals); and subsequently, with a high degree of accuracy, to age the animals after shooting in order to mark off the pyramid against the plan, as the plan becomes accomplished.

Continuing over the years we shall end up with a pyramid (as shown in Fig A1). In this pyramid each shooting year is depicted by a different colour and we have been building it up every year from the line marked 'start'. The ages of animals at the time are shown between the blocks of 'stags' and 'hinds'. Every subsequent year a new horizontal line is added at the bottom depicting the numbers of calves, and each subsequent colour shows the accomplished shooting plan for that year.

The current year's age structure is shown at the edge of the 'stags' block.

An approach similar in concept, but simpler in detail and requiring a lower degree of skill in ageing the animals, can be used by grouping the ages into appropriate blocks. We can then present it as a table of percentages, working suitable proportions in percentage values to each group corresponding with age groupings of calves, young animals, mature and old, and making a distinction between good and poor beasts (Fig A6).

Finally we ought to have another look at the results of a high ratio of hinds to stags.

STAGS	YOUNG under 3 years	MATURE 3–10 years	OLD over 10 years
Good	preserve	preserve	shoot
	— 40% —	— 47% —	— 13% —
Poor	shoot at an early age		

HINDS	under 3 years	3–8/9 years	over 8/9 years
Good	preserve in right numbers		shoot unless herd leading
	— 40% —	— 55% —	— 5% —
Poor	shoot at an early age		

A6   Culling guide, related to quality and age

Let us return to our ground with the initial capacity of 300 head and the calving rate of 40 per cent by the spring count; our age span is still fifteen years and the sex ratio at the outset 1:1, giving us a distribution of 150 animals of each sex.

Our 150 hinds will produce 60 calves. Our structure, however, requires only 40 (to maintain our correct age distribution in the pyramid). We therefore have 20 surplus calves.

If we do not cull this surplus of calves and allow our stock to grow, by the time the hinds have reached the number of 200 the annual increase will be 80 calves, and therefore 40 surplus calves.

If our starting stock is at a ratio not of 1:1 but of 1:1·5, we shall have 180 hinds, which will produce 72 calves, or 32 surplus, whereas at the ratio of 1:2, 200 hinds will produce 80 calves, or 40 too many. If we did no culling at all and had a natural survival rate as the only controller of numbers, within one generation (about five years in red deer) our stock would double with the ratio of 1:1, treble at 1:1·5 and quadruple at 1:2. This is the danger which will loom over us if the ratios and the culling are not carefully adjusted.

It is not difficult to imagine the effect on the condition of our deer if the ground capable of sustaining 300 head was to carry double or even treble that number.

GENERAL CONSIDERATIONS OF DEER ECONOMICS*

(Based on paper delivered 1970)

This paper considers certain aspects of 'deer economics'.

DEER AS AN ASSET

As an asset, the value of deer can be seen in two categories:

1 As potential sporting value.
2 As the annual return for venison sold (or consumed).

SPORTING VALUE

Under this heading, we look at the sport which the animals should offer within the annual shooting plan, and therefore at the potential value of the sporting rights if these were let. In consequence, as the stag presents a potential antler trophy, it holds a higher value than a hind—even though, as an object of the stalk, both may provide the same type of sport.

VENISON PRODUCTION

Here, we wish to crop the deer at the time of life when their weight is at its highest; ie, when body development has reached its peak and before the general deterioration in quality—due to age—has started.

* Appendices 5–8 are based upon the papers presented by the author annually to a co-operating group of Scottish estate owners. The group (lairds, factors and keepers) meets once a year to consider their general policy and the 'tactics' for the ensuing stalking season. These papers are distributed in advance to all those attending the meetings.

Appendix 5

OPTIMAL CROPPING AGE

To a large extent, both interests can be met under this heading within a very small margin of difference.

The body development of deer can be represented as in Fig A7.

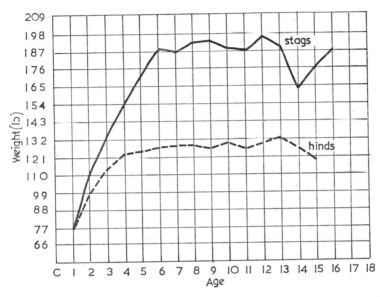

A7 Body development in relation to age (based on *Red Deer Research in Scotland*, Progress Report 1, August 1967)

On the basis of this graph, therefore, one could say that the optimal cropping ages are:

Stags — 6–12 years;
Hinds — 4–14 years.

Additionally, if we were to graph the main assets of each sex—ie, stags' antler development and hinds' calf-bearing—we would obtain a picture as shown in Fig A8.

It would follow, therefore, that—in the interests of economics—the execution of the shooting plan should be so adjusted as to allow for a high crop of animals at the upper age bracket of their

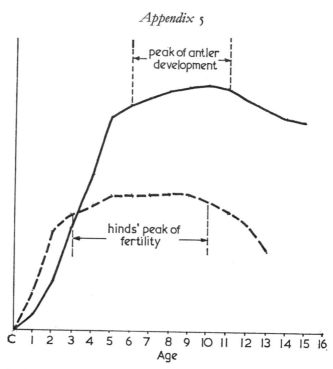

A8 Antler and fertility development in relation to age (based on B. Mitchell, *Deer*, January 1970; de Nahlik, *Wild Deer*; Raesefeld, ed. Vorreyer, *Das Rotwild*)

respective optimal development, thus allowing for full propagation at the ages of full maturity. However, for the sake of stock improvement, it is necessary to crop the animals which show little or no promise, and this consideration must be the overriding criterion.

Thus an important facet of deer management arises: the question of recognition—the ability to define on sight a good animal, distinguish it from a poor one, assess the value as stock and decide its age—all to be done before deciding whether or not to shoot.

The basic need for recognition is evident and, although as a task it may appear to produce a problem, in practice it presents only a small difficulty, provided that, as a matter of routine with both stags and hinds, the age of the animal having been estimated when it was alive and on the hoof, is then checked—and possibly reconsidered—through close examination of the jaws immediately the animal has been shot. By these means, a mental comparison can be made between the age as assessed by bodily appearance and the more accurate assessment on the basis of tooth formation.

There should be no difficulty in distinguishing between a young stag (of, say, 2 3 years) with an antler which carries a good potential, and an older and poorer stag (of, say, 5–6 years) with an antler which for its age is inadequately developed—provided due note is taken of the bodily appearance of the animal.

The problems of hind recognition are, of course, that much greater, especially if one considers such factors as whether the hind is barren or having a 2/3 yearly 'rest' period; whether it is a good mother; and whether it is a producer of strong calves.

In consequence, the degree of error in hind recognition must be accepted as potentially greater than that in stag recognition, especially if one adds the problem of the weather factor during the hind shooting season. All the more reason, perhaps, why earlier rather than later hind cropping should be encouraged.

CROP RECORD 1968
The figures provided by the 1968 season, as presented in Fig A9, suggest that the age bracket covered by the executed shooting plan is too low; the need therefore arises for the shifting of the shooting selection towards older animals.

It may be argued that the animals should be shot as soon as it is established that they are of no value for bloodstock purposes, and this argument is perfectly valid; however, while a high proportion of poor, older animals remain on the hill, at the peak of their fertility, they must represent a higher priority in the execution of the shooting plan.

SEX RATIOS
For some time now, sex ratio has been discussed with the aim of deciding the need (or desirability) of adjusting it to somewhere in the region of 1:1.

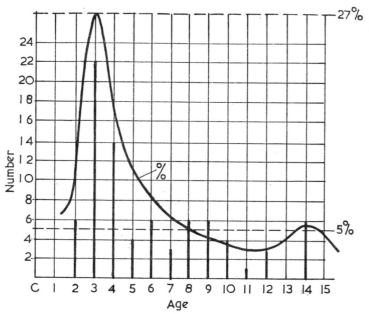

AGE DISTRIBUTION OF STAGS
SHOT - SEASON 1968
(All estates)

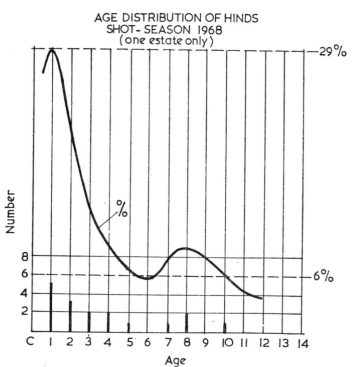

AGE DISTRIBUTION OF HINDS
SHOT - SEASON 1968
(one estate only)

A9

The figures for the estate group are as follows:

	Stags	Hinds	Calves	Stags:Hinds
1963	275	468	222	1:1·7
1964	315	499	246	1:1·6
1965	577	805	423	1:1·4
1966	435	758	392	1:1·7
1967	478	666	366	1:1·4
1968	489	740	346	1:1·5
1969	414	785	388	1:1·9
1970	446	754	328	1:1·6

If we adopted the continental method of assessing the sex ratios, ie, counting stags in relation to hinds *plus* calves, we would have:

	Stags	Hinds	Stags:Hinds/Calves
1963	275	690	1:2·5
1964	315	745	1:2·4
1965	577	1,228	1:2·1
1966	435	1,150	1:2·7
1967	478	1,032	1:2·2
1968	489	1,086	1:2·2
1969	414	1,173	1:2·8
1970	446	1,082	1:2·4

It is interesting to note that the Rhum experiments are based on the ratio of 1:1 (stags plus male calves: hinds plus female calves) and use approximately the same method of assessing as the first set of figures above.

I would rather not get involved in justification of a sex ratio of 1:1 as being desirable (although I do strongly believe that such a ratio is desirable). I should like to point out the following, however:

1 Most forests on the Continent, and several in Scotland (eg, Glenfiddich) have found that the ratio of 1:1 provides good breeding and stock conditions.

2 Most research reports are based on stocks which are maintained at the ratio of 1:1.

3 As an asset, a stag must be accepted as being of higher value than a hind—therefore the greater the stock of stags, the greater the economic value of the stock.

CONCLUSION

There is a need for greater effort towards attaining accuracy in deer recognition in order to improve deer management and sporting and economic interests of the deer forests. This is a task which affects all levels of the hierarchy—lairds and stalkers, factors and stalking guests.

At the same time, in order to formulate the aims of the Deer Committee and those of the individual lairds, a universally acceptable policy regarding the size of deer stock, and the breakdown of the sex ratio, on the island should be considered.

BALANCE OF SEX RATIO IN DEER ECONOMICS

(Based on paper delivered 1971)

Last year, in my paper to the Committee, I discussed certain aspects of 'deer economics', giving an overall view of the problem. This year I should like to discuss the important fact of balancing the economy, namely the sex ratio.

REVENUE

It is clear that an important objective of an estate these days must be to optimise the return from 'the hill'. Whether this return is through sheep, cattle, hill farming, grouse or deer is, in the sense of economics, a secondary consideration. In this paper I do not propose to compare the return from these sources but to concentrate purely on deer and to consider how to obtain the highest possible return from deer stalking.

DEER AS AN ASSET

As an asset, deer can be considered from several points of view.

VENISON

The price of venison fluctuates; apart from the seasonal fluctuation, the year-to-year changes follow the pattern of demand. The demand has been rising, possibly as a result of the growth of the continental markets, possibly as a result of the steady increase of meat prices on the home market. It is difficult to forecast whether our entry 'into Europe' will affect the trends; what is fairly certain, however, is that upon entry into the Common Market the price of meat will increase and with it should increase the price of venison. It also seems that the home market demand is increasing. Pound for pound, venison from a hind or stag fetches the same price and the difference therefore between the two, from the point of view of the revenue, is the weight of the beast; thus a stag is a more valuable beast than a hind.

SPORT

There are two considerations in this field. Scottish stalking is unique and, as sport, unequalled. Against this, the Scottish antler is considerably smaller than the continental one or even the Lakeland or English (Norfolk or West Country). Furthermore, even where a good stag is found in Scotland, a chance of killing one without damaging the herd is small, because the number of good stags is small. On the other hand, there is an ever-increasing demand for leisure among the population of Britain and with it the return from stalking has a growing potential which may be further enhanced by an improvement of the quality of antlers to a degree where they become a treasured (even if smaller) trophy for British or continental (or American) sportsmen. In general terms, a stag represents greater value to a stalker than a hind and therefore is a greater potential revenue-earner than a hind.

A first-class stag on the Continent, in Rumania, Hungary or Yugoslavia, can be secured for something in excess of £833–£1,250, against hind stalking for which a fee of £12·50–£20·50 is normally demanded. The Scottish prices today stand at £20–£30 for a stag and £5–£10 for a hind (indeed, some estates offer hind-stalking free), while the better-stock estates charge £30–£40 for a stag.

BY-PRODUCTS

At present the by-products from deer—skins, livers, etc—bring little or no revenue to the estate in spite of the fact that there is, as yet, an unexplored market in this country for them.

Appendix 6

REVENUE

Forgetting by-products, however, the basic and important considerations are:

Number of animals to be taken per year.
Price of venison.
Value of deer stalking.

Of these three, the second is common to both sexes and is not controllable by the estate, whereas the first and third can be at least influenced by the estate and the policy it pursues.

As we all know, the numbers of animals to be taken each year clearly must be related to the number of deer that can be carried on the land. Here the estate policies have to decide on other uses of land and the proportion allotted to deer, feeding in winter, and the proportion of hinds to stags (and therefore the proportion that can be taken off the hill each season). From the point of view of economics, the ratio of 1:1 seems to produce the highest economic return in a defined size of 'crop' as is suggested in Table A1 and Fig A10. Apart from the economics, it is accepted that this ratio provides the best breeding results.

Value of deer as sport (stalking) also differs; here the main criterion is the size and excellence of antler. At the moment the average price for stag stalking in Scotland is approximately £20–£30, but if antlers of twelve points or more could be guaranteed or even promised as possible or likely trophy, a higher price might be obtained. Against this, hind stalking, while excellent sport, carries a lower value and some estates offer it free. Thus a policy which aims at improvement of antler should result in increasing the potential revenue from the sport. At the same time, such a policy will improve the health and well-being of the beasts and therefore must result in increased body weights, thus increasing the revenue from venison. In simple terms, the animal improvement policy means provision of weather shelter, accessible water, and above all appropriate quality and quantity of food especially during antler-forming and gestation periods. Where experiments with feeding have been seriously undertaken, results of some

importance have been observed, especially if careful selective
shooting is also strictly pursued.

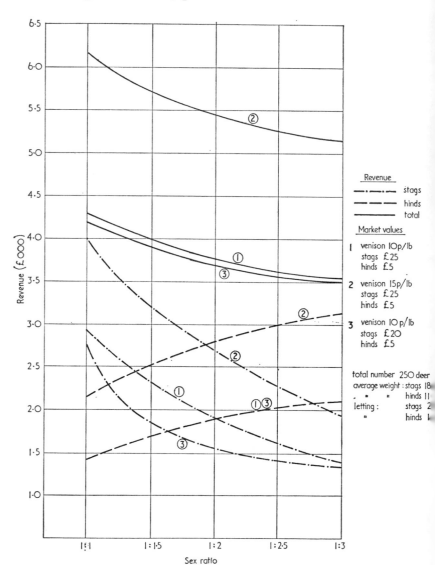

A10   Revenue to sex ratio relationship

Appendix 6

DEER VERSUS OTHER FARMING INTERESTS

The question which so far remains unresolved is the competition which deer have to face from other farming interests, both in the care afforded to them and the competition they face from other animals and interests on the hill; the latter is really a matter of density of animals on the hill versus the food they can find in their natural surroundings. A great deal of study has been devoted to the solution of these problems but unfortunately so far no clear results are available. It has been established that deer's rate of food conversion is higher than any other animals'; thus the return from feeding naturally or artificially is higher in deer than in the animals which one tends to find on the hill. The question of density could be at least partially solved if we were able to establish with a degree of certainty such variables as the ideal deer density on a given land, or a 'conversion' between the hill sheep or cattle and deer, ie, calculate how many more deer one could successfully maintain on the hill if one were to eliminate the sheep. The information here is of mixed value. The Nature Conservancy on Rhum, having eliminated the sheep, finds that there is little difference in deer with the exception that there might be a marginal improvement in health. On the other hand, recent experiments carried out in other parts of Scotland suggest that the results of devoting the hill to deer only can result in startling improvements, especially if accompanied by careful, well-timed and balanced feeding. Even the basic question of deer density is unclear. Scotland varies between 23 and 39 acres per head of deer, the Continent recommends 50–150 and sometimes even more; on the Continent, however, an important criterion is the damage to forest at high densities of deer.

Looking at the three estates here by Scottish standards, the deer-to-acreage ratio works out at about 28 acres per head but is accompanied by a pretty high sheep population. One could accept, therefore, that if sheep were eliminated a greater deer population could be carried, and to that end a ratio based on weights could be used (1 deer = approximately 3–4 sheep).

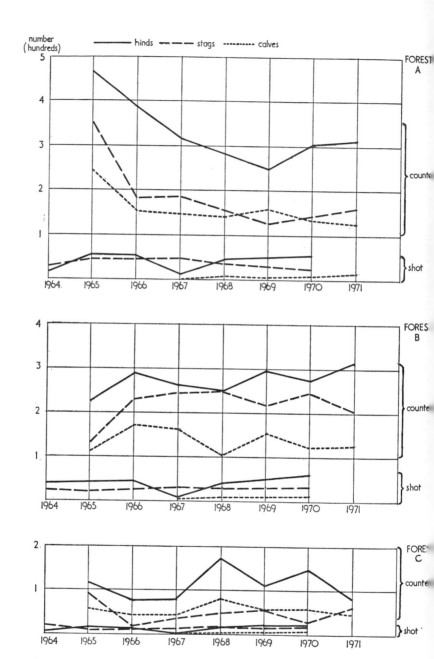

A11 Individual forests within group 'X'

CONCLUSION

The indications are that the various policies so far adopted on the island are paying off. There is little doubt that the heads are improving and the weight of the animals is also increasing. But a serious look is needed at the question of economics.

I submit that the attached Table A1 and Fig A10 conclusively suggest that we ought to aim at a sex ratio of 1:1, because at that ratio the return on deer is highest. Such a ratio could be achieved

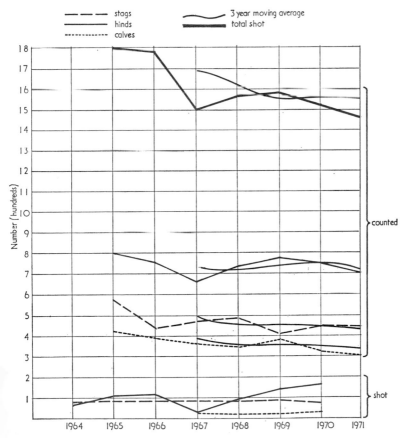

A12 'X' group of forests. Deer counted and shot (with 3-year moving averages)

TABLE A1
REVENUE/SEX RATIO
Annual shooting plan (n = 250)
Average weights used: stags 180lb; hinds 110lb

Market	Ratio	No of stags	Sale of venison £	Stalking £	Revenue (Stags) £	No of hinds	Sale of venison £	Stalking £	Revenue £	Revenue grand total £
Venison 10p @ £25	1:1	125	2,250	625	2,875	125	1,430	30	1,460	4,335
stags 20% @ £25	1:1·5	100	1,800	500	2,300	150	1,650	35	1,685	3,985
hinds 5% @ £5	1:2	83	1,490	425	1,915	167	1,840	40	1,880	3,795
	1:2·5	72	1,295	350	1,645	178	1,960	45	2,005	3,650
1	1:3	62	1,115	300	1,415	188	2,070	50	2,120	3,535
Venison 15p	1:1	125	3,375	625	4,000	125	2,145	30	2,175	6,175
stags 20% @ £25	1:1·5	100	2,700	500	3,200	150	2,475	35	2,510	5,710
hinds 5% @ £5	1:2	83	2,235	425	2,660	167	2,760	40	2,800	5,460
	1:2·5	72	1,942	350	2,292	178	2,940	45	2,985	5,277
2	1:3	62	1,672	300	1,972	188	3,105	50	3,155	5,127
Venison 10p	1:1	125	2,250	500	2,750	125	1,430	30	1,460	4,210
stags 20% @ £20	1:1·5	100	1,800	400	2,200	150	1,650	35	1,680	3,885
hinds 5% @ £5	1:2	83	1,490	340	1,830	167	1,840	40	1,880	3,710
	1:2·5	72	1,295	280	1,575	178	1,960	45	2,005	3,580
3	1:3	62	1,115	240	1,355	188	2,070	50	2,120	3,475

Note Graphical presentation of this table is in Fig A10.

in a comparatively short time: in three years by increasing the quota of hinds to about 200 (180 last year), maintaining the quota of stags at about 90 and of calves at about 40, or by increasing the quota of hinds to 230, decreasing the quota of stags to about 70 (and maintaining the quota of calves at 40) with an overall result of decreasing the number of beasts by about 100 and almost reaching sex parity in two years. Once near-parity has been reached, the shooting of equal numbers of stags and hinds (in approximation) and therefore optimisation of return should be possible. Having achieved parity of sexes, adjustment of the deer population up or down would not present a large problem. Figs A11 and A12 represent graphically the year by year deer population level, and the level of shooting as related to each estate (A11) and all estates combined (A12).

SEX RATIO AND CULLING OF CALVES

(Based on paper delivered 1973)

Every year, since I started to help and advise on deer management, I have advocated adoption of an agreed policy concerning the principles upon which deer management should be based and developed.

My papers to the Deer Committee considered a number of issues of a general and particular nature and recommended courses of action which I considered appropriate. Whilst some recommendations have been accepted and put into operation, the general policy has never been formally agreed, and in the absence of such guidance my advice has always been aimed at the achievement of certain defined objectives, namely:

1 To eliminate poor stock.
2 To adjust the numbers so as to achieve a density of 1 head to 30 acres as the highest density acceptable.
3 To reduce the sex ratio to approximately 1:1.

In the absence of objections to these objectives, my recommendations pursued these aims by setting the targets in the sequence of annual shooting plans, selection principles, etc. The stipulated targets have, to a large degree, been successfully reached inasmuch as the quality of the beasts has improved abreast of the lower density of deer on the ground, the sex ratio has come closer to 1:1. In the last few months, however, some disquiet has been voiced on account of the decreased population and the changing sex ratio, and a change in the general policy has been suggested. This paper attempts to defend the validity of the 1:1 sex ratio and the need for control of calf numbers. I would have liked to include in it another important topic, that of deer density, because it is also an issue of some gravity; however, to date, little published authoritative information is available on the subject of desirable deer density in Britain. The Red Deer Commission, in its reports, talks in terms of 30 acres per head but this is no more than a general guideline and is not supported. Some work is in progress in this field and results may become available in some months, maybe a year; there is, of course, an abundance of material published on the Continent, related to both rich and poor food areas, but none of the areas are as poor in nutritious values as Scotland. In view of the general reluctance to accept the applicability of the continental data to Scottish conditions, I do not propose to labour this point. However, it is worth mentioning that, in 1962, when the deer population of Estate A was 351 head (146 stags, 148 hinds—therefore a ratio of 1:1—and 57 calves), as counted by the Red Deer Commission, the Commission advised that 'it would be unwise, in the Commission's view, to allow the deer stock to be increased, since such increase would be at the expense of quality'.

The Commission agreed, however, that its figures may have been low, on account of weather conditions at the time of counting; furthermore, at the time 3,600 sheep—and in summer 200 cattle—used the hill.

So, to ensure viability of figures, let us take the following year's count and compare these with the present, showing the three major estates, as in Table A2.

TABLE A2

DEER HOLDING ON ESTATE GROUP 'X', 1963 AND 1973

Estate	Deer acres	1963				1973			
		Stags	Hinds	Calves	Total	Stags	Hinds	Calves	Total
A	16,000	114	230	109	354	168	296	147	611
B	12,000	144	155	80	379	216	255	134	605
C	8,000	17	83	33	133	67	61	35	163
	36,000	275	468	222	965	451	612	316	1,379

Density: 1963—39 acres per head; 1973—26 acres per head.

Appendix 7

Sex ratio and control of calves are other issues completely. In these fields specific analyses can be made and alternative policies considered; in such considerations, however, certain parameters and constraints have to be accepted, but these do not change the validity of the main principles.

In discussing sex ratio I will refer on occasion to a graphical presentation of the problem as shown in Fig A13. In such presentation the population is graphed as a triangular pyramid; its height (or vertical axis) represents the age, the base (or the horizontal axis), the numbers of animals, with the bottom line therefore representing the number of calves. The calves outside the triangle are animals surplus to need. The left-hand side of the triangle are the male animals and the right side the females. Each square represents ten beasts, and each horizontal line of squares an age group. The slope of the arms is therefore the rate at which the population size, related to age, decreases as a result of natural mortality and shooting. If, therefore, the area of the pyramid is known, this being the total of the population, and the age structure is also known—for we know how long the animals live— we can establish the base which represents the number of calves; this is controlled now by two other variables following the formula of the area of the triangle.

$$\text{Area} = \tfrac{1}{2}\,\text{base} \times \text{height}$$

$$\therefore \text{Base} = \frac{\text{area}}{\tfrac{1}{2}\,\text{height}}\text{or:}$$

$$\text{Calves required} = \frac{\text{total population}}{\tfrac{1}{2}\,\text{age span}}$$

For the purpose of this calculation I am taking the life span of deer as being fourteen years, ie, the age of the older beasts which have been found in this locality.

The next parameter used is that of calving rate related to March counts which I take as being 42 per cent of hind population across the age bands. I have been using in my calculations, over the past six years, rates of 40 per cent and 45 per cent and have found that my prognoses have been fairly accurate, falling usually between these two figures, when accompanied by a mortality due to natural and other causes (shooting apart) at the level of 5 per cent. One could adjust these two variables, compensating for a change in one by appropriate change in the other: I maintain, however, that the reported findings of dead animals and reported suspected poachings do not warrant the increase of rate of 5 per cent.

The Deer Count of 1973 is represented graphically in Fig A13 and Tables A3–A6; the counted number of calves (316) does, however, represent the rate of 52 per cent which is high and suggests therefore either that there has been an overcount or that there has been an unusually high winter survival. Just as much, therefore, as in 1972 we undercounted (as proved by 1973 count), so I suggest that this year calves were overcounted and as a result I am using a figure corresponding to 42 per cent calving rate as being statistically valid. For these reasons the figures used in Table A7 and in most of the further discussion are: stags 451; hinds 612 (total adults 1,063); calves 257 (42 per cent of hinds).

The third parameter I am using is the sex ratio among the calves. There is increasingly strong evidence, based on the experiences gained by the Nature Conservancy on Rhum, The Rowett Institute and in the number of calf-tagging exercises performed by the Red Deer Commission, that the sex ratio among the calves is about 1:1. There is proof, however, that the survival rate of young male beasts up to the age of two or three years is slightly lower than that of females, and that, at the other end of the scale, the survival rate of older hinds is lower than that of stags; thus, over the life span, the *natural* sex ratio would be about 1:1.

To maintain a steady level of population of deer we have to 'adjust' the numbers every year by a figure corresponding to the natural increase; I use the word 'adjust' because this is a combination of natural mortality and planned shooting. To maintain the overall population, therefore, at a constant level, we would have to adjust by 257 beasts (42 per cent of 612 hinds); the natural mortality will take 5 per cent of the population of 1,320 (612 hinds, 451 stags and 257 calves), ie, 66 beasts, thus leaving 191 to be shot.

Some advocates of policy change talk in terms of a sex ratio of

1:3. Table A3 considers what happens at various sex ratios, taking the present number of adult beasts as the basis of our calculation.

TABLE A3

SHOOTING PLAN RELATED TO VARIOUS SEX RATIOS

	Present ratio of 1:1·3	1:1	1:2	1:3
Stags	451	534	356	267
Hinds	612	534	712	801
Total adults	1,063	1,068	1,068	1,068
Calves as 42% of hinds	257	224	299	336
Total population	1,320	1,292	1,367	1,404
Mortality @ 5%	66	64	68	70
Shooting target* (ie, no of calves less mortality)	191	160	231	266
Resulting population†	1,063	1,068	1,068	1,068
Shooting as % of population	14	12·5	17	19

* Aimed at maintaining a constant level of deer population.

† Ie the same as the number of adult animals before the shooting season.

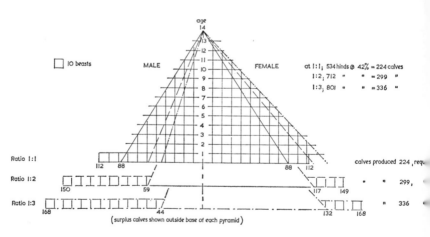

A13   Relationship between sex ratio and calving established at steady population of 1,063 *adult* animals

Let us consider in turn (Table A4) how many calves should be shot each year in order to maintain a steady population and equitable age distribution in the deer herds as suggested by Fig A13.

TABLE A4

CALF SHOOTING AT VARIOUS SEX RATIOS

	At present *ratio of* 1:1·3	1:1	1:2	1:3
Calves @ 42%	257	224	299	336
Calculated number of calves needed	176	176	176	176
Calves mortality at 5%	13	11	15	17
Calves surplus to be shot	68	37	108	143

If no calves were to be shot for *one year*, the situation at various ratios would be as shown in Table A5.

TABLE A5

SHOOTING PLAN WITH MORATORIUM ON CALF-SHOOTING

FOR ONE YEAR

	At present *ratio of* 1:1·3	1:1	1:2	1:3
Calves at 42%	257	224	299	336
Less 1 year mortality @ 5%	13	11	15	17
Calves remaining (or adults to be shot during year)	244	213	284	319
Shooting as % of adult population	23	20	27·5	33

If no calves were to be shot for two years (which, as some suggest, would bring a better return from venison and would decrease the problems of selection of young beasts to be shot), the situation would be as shown in Table A6.

TABLE A6

SHOOTING PLAN WITH MORATORIUM ON SHOOTING YOUNG DEER (CALVES AND YEARLINGS)

	At present ratio of 1:1·3	1:1	1:2	1:3
Calves year 1	257	224	299	336
less mortality	13	11	15	17
Calves ex-year 1	244	213	284	319
Calves year 2	257	224	299	336
Total young animals	501	437	583	655
Total deer holding (including young)	1,325	1,292	1,367	1,404
Shootable animals above 2 years old	824	855	784	749
Shoot annual increase (ex-year 1)	244	213	284	319
Adult 'survivors'	580	642	500	430
Therefore adults shot as %	29·5	25	36	43

The conclusions which can be drawn, from both the discussions and the figures quoted, are self-evident: they can be summarised as follows:

1 In order to allow for a graded age distribution at all age levels, which gives us a proportion of mature beasts, only a limited number of calves is required; the number is closely related to the overall holding capacity of the ground.

2 As sex ratio increases, so the number of animals to be shot increases, if the overall holding is to be maintained at a steady level; however, the increase in shooting is absorbed wholly by calf shooting and *not* by shooting mature animals.

3 The policy of not shooting calves for *two* years, even with sex ratio of 1:1, would result in a *quarter* of the adult population having to be shot; at ratio of 1:2 *one third*, and at 1:3 nearly *half* thus precluding a chance of survival to full maturity by any number of animals. Therefore, whilst a ratio of 1:3 and even higher may be tenable in deer *farming*, under carefully controlled conditions, it is untenable in wild hill deer.

4 A high proportion of revenue is derived from deer stalking, where stags are more valuable and more easily marketable than hinds. Furthermore, stags produce more venison; hence the value of stags is higher (see Table A7).

TABLE A7
REVENUE: SEX RATIO RELATIONSHIP

(As related to a shooting plan of 200 adult beasts. Assumed weights: stags—180lb; hinds—110lb.)

Assumptions	Sex ratio	Number shot	Sale of venison £	Stalking value £	Total revenue £	Number shot	Sale of venison £	Stalking value £	Total revenue £	Grand Total £
Venison	1:1	100	2,700	4,000	6,700	100	1,650	200	1,850	8,550
15p/lb	1:1·5	80	2,160	3,200	5,360	120	1,980	240	2,220	7,580
Stalking	1:2	67	1,809	2,680	4,489	133	2,194	270	2,464	6,953
stags £40										
all let	1:2·5	57	1,539	2,280	3,819	142	2,343	290	2,633	6,452
Hinds	1:3	50	1,350	2,000	3,350	150	2,475	300	2,775	6,125
£10										
20% let										
Venison	1:1	100	3,600	4,000	7,600	100	2,200	200	2,400	10,000
20p/lb	1:1·5	80	2,880	3,200	6,080	120	2,640	240	2,880	8,960
Stalking	1:2	67	2,412	2,680	5,092	133	2,926	270	3,196	8,288
as above	1:2·5	57	2,052	2,280	4,332	142	3,124	280	3,414	7,746
	1:3	50	1,800	2,000	3,800	150	3,300	300	3,600	7,400
Venison	1:1	100	7,200	4,000	11,200	100	4,400	200	4,600	15,800
40p/lb	1:1·5	80	5,760	3,200	8,960	120	5,280	240	5,520	14,480
Stalking	1:2	67	4,824	2,680	7,504	133	5,852	270	6,122	13,626
as above	1:2·5	57	4,104	2,280	6,384	142	6,248	280	6,528	12,912
	1:3	50	3,600	2,000	5,600	150	6,600	300	6,900	12,500

We have had the experience in the last few years of the amount of effort needed to control the overall numbers and to adjust the sex ratio to approximately 1:1. It meant a heavy, and carefully selective and controlled, shooting plan which had to be followed for several years. An adjustment 'the other way', away from 1:1 ratio, is by comparison easy; one has to shoot fewer hinds and maintain the same level of stag shooting, and as a result the hind population will increase in no time. Thus a decision to change either the sex ratio, or cut the calf shooting, or increase the overall population should not be taken lightly—remembering that all these will affect the quality of the beasts in an adverse manner.

OTHER INCOME FROM DEER

An investigation carried out recently suggests that, apart from venison and sporting letting, there is an additional revenue from deer stalking which at present, in most areas, is regarded as 'Keeper's Perks'. The prices which can be obtained on the market and the potential income from these commodities can be stipulated as follows:

	Keeper's price	Potential	Remarks
Liver	20p/lb	20p/lb	If the market could
Hearts	20p/lb	20p/lb	be stimulated, the
Kidneys	5p/lb	5p/lb	prices should increase by up to 50%
Skins	30p each	50–60p	Good skins are no more than from 50% of animals shot
Tusks	£1·50–£2·00 per pair	£2·00–£2·50	Exported 100%
Antlers	5p/lb	10p/lb	more

If one takes these commodities as a total per animal, the value per beast, apart from the antlers, could be in the region of £2·50 at 'keeper's price'. If this value was to be added to the model in Appendix 4, it could make a considerable difference to the planning of land utilisation.

One could assume that, if a well-established market for the by-products could be found or created, it would be worthwhile 'buying-out' the keepers' perks either by a down payment or in the form of an addition to their wages, for the market demand for these could be enlarged and properly stimulated. For those who doubt this suggestion, all one can say is, that not many years ago the market value of venison was but a fraction of the present value, new markets having been opened by enterprising industrialists.

COMPARISON OF DEER AND SHEEP

A variety of attempts have so far been made to establish a comparative evaluation of deer versus sheep. The calculations presented below are based on the hypothesis presented by F. Vorreyer, one of the foremost West German experts and author of several works on deer ecology; these suggest that one red deer can be equated with three sheep—the basis of equation being the comparative food consumption by these animals. Even if this hypothesis is refuted and another preferred, a system similar to the one used below can still be applied and different set figures be arrived at.

Estate 'X' previously mentioned in the text

1 *Sample income* from 100-ewe flock per annum

80% lambing	@ £4	£320	
100 fleeces	@ £1	£100	
Sheep subsidy	@ £1	£100	
			£520

2 *Less*

Shepherding (based on a 500-ewe flock)	£200	
Variable cost:		
Veterinary fees etc @ 40p per head	£40	
Feeding @ 25p	£25	
Marketing and transport	£15	
Ram replacement @ 1½p per head	£60	
		£340

Net income per 100 ewes	£180

Gross income per ewe	£5·20
Net income per ewe	£1·80

DEER

On the other hand, the same estate carried a stock of 1,589 head of deer and in 1970 culled 288 beasts distributed as follows: stags 100; hinds 155; calves 33.

The income from deer calculated at 1970 prices—venison at 17·5p per lb, sporting letting potential at £20 per stag and £10 per hind—is:

1 Venison:	Stags	100 @	140lb @ 17·5p	£2,450	
	Hinds	155 @	78lb @ 17·5p	£2,116	
	Calves	33 @	30lb @ 17·5p	£173	
					£4,739
2 Stalking:	Stags	100 @ £20		£2,000	
	Hinds	155 @ £10		£1,150	
					£3,550
	Gross income				£8,289

Using the 'Vorreyer' hypothesis of 1 deer = 3 sheep, we can now equate the gross income from deer to that from sheep: 100 sheep = 33·33 deer, and therefore:

1 Venison:
$$\frac{33 \cdot 33 \text{ (deer equivalent of 100 sheep)}}{1,589 \text{ (deer holding on the ground)}} \times £4,739 \text{ (revenue from venison)} = £99 \cdot 40$$

2 Sporting letting:
$$\frac{33 \cdot 33 \text{ (deer equivalent of 100 sheep)}}{1,589 \text{ (deer holding on the ground)}} \times £3,550 \text{ (revenue from letting)} = £74 \cdot 46$$

Revenue from 100 sheep equivalent (33·33 deer)   £173·86

However, if the ratio of stags to hinds had been adjusted to 1:1 and therefore culling had been on a 1:1 basis:

1 Venison:				
	127 stags	@ 140lb @ 17·5p	£3,111	
	128 hinds	@ 78lb @ 17·5p	£1,747	
	33 calves	@ 30lb @ 17·5p	£173	
				£5,031·00

2 Sporting letting:

127 stags @ £20	£2,540	
128 hinds @ £10	£1,280	£3820·00

Gross income	£8,851·00

These figures can now be equated to a 100-ewe flock by the method applied above, giving:

Venison	£105·55
Sporting letting	£80·10

Gross income from 33·33 red deer	£185·65 (or approx
(equivalent to 100 sheep)	7% increase)

A study of a sample of estates will allow a calculation of the net income from 33·33 deer, as an equivalent to 100 sheep:

1 Income from 33·33 deer

Venison	£99·40	
Sporting letting	£74·46	
		£173·86

2 Less fixed costs (based on holding of 1,500 deer)

keepering	£21·98	
variable costs:		
feeding	£21·98	
transport, etc	£6·78	
		£50·74

Net income	£123·12

Gross income from 33·33 deer—per head		
(100 sheep equivalent)	of sheep	£1·73
Net income from 33·33 deer —per head		
(100 sheep equivalent)	of sheep	£1·23

Overtly, on this calculation, using the figures of Estate 'X', the income from deer seems to be lower than that from sheep; however:

1 (a) If the sheep subsidy was to be halved:
   Gross income per ewe   £4·70
   Net income per ewe   £1·30
   (b) In the event of the sheep subsidy being withdrawn:
   Gross income per ewe   £4·20
   Net income per ewe   £0·80

2 If the sex ratio of adult deer was adjusted to 1:1 and resulted in 1:1 culling of stags and hinds and an increase in revenue in the region of 7 per cent was reached, the income would change to:
   Gross income from deer in 'sheep equivalent' £1·85 per head of sheep
   Net income from deer in 'sheep equivalent'   £1·36 per head of sheep

3 If the deer are fed at the suggested rate, for which allowance is made in the overheads quoted above ('feeding of 33·33 deer £21·98' which equals £1,000 for 1,500 deer), an improvement in the return could be expected in both the carcass weights and antler values, within say five years, in the region of 10 per cent, putting a conservative estimate on it. Taking a 10 per cent improvement:
   Gross income from deer in 'sheep equivalent' £1·73 + 17p = £1·90 per sheep
   Net income   £1·23 + 17p = £1·40

4 If allowance were made for improvement in the general condition of deer, *and the stock were adjusted to* 1:1 *ratio*, the two-fold benefit from increased weight and more stags to be shot would produce:
   Gross income from deer in 'sheep equivalent' £2·02 per head of sheep
   Net income   £1·52

5 Finally, if Dr Leckie's figures for stalking fees as £50 per stag are accepted, and they do not seem unlikely, and the venison price remained at the present level:
   Gross income from deer in 'sheep equivalent' £2·65 per head of sheep
   Net income   £2·15

In the comparative costing of sheep versus deer, instead of taking figures provided by Estate 'X', one can use those published

in the August 1970 issue of *Livestock Farming* to test the income
from sheep; the figures published were as follows:

		Upland sheep £		*Hill sheep* £
Income:				
Lambing		8·80		2·55
Cast ewes		—		70
Wool		1·20		1·15
Subsidy		70		1·20
		10·70		5·60
Variable costs:				
Depreciation	(per ewe)	2·10	(per ram)	20
Feeding (concentrates)		40		55
Vet fees and medicines		25		20
Marketing and transport		30		20
Forage		1·60		10
Fixed costs:				
Labour (including farm help)		2·65		2·25
Power and machinery		70		40
Miscellaneous expenses		50		40
Rent		1·00		35
		9·50		4·65
Income per head		10·70		5·60
Costs per head		9·50		4·65
Net profit per head		1·20		0·95

The important conclusion which can be drawn from the figures
quoted is that, whilst the profitability from sheep may be marginally below or above that from deer, deer have much under-
developed potential, whereas sheep seem to be, if anything, on
the decline. Furthermore, the sheep profitability rests to a degree
on the sheep subsidy. Against this if an effort was made on a
national basis to improve hill deer, aiming at higher carcass
weights (say thirteen stone for a stag and nine stone for a hind as

an average), such increases in weights should also produce an improvement in the value of stag stalking, and under such circumstances Dr Leckie's figure of £50 per stag is not only feasible but, by the standard charges outside Britain, low. There is no doubt that the £1,000 antlers of Hungarian or Yugoslavian standards are unlikely to materialise, but an average good twelve-pointer, backed by the unique value of Scottish stalking, should and could realise a capitation fee of £100.

REFERENCES

1 Waldo, C. M., and Wislocki, G. B. 'Observations on shedding of antlers of Virginia Deer', *American Journal of Anatomy* (1951)

2 Chaplin, R. 'Reproduction in British Deer', *Sunday Times* (1960)

3 Eidman, H. 'Untersuchungen am Gebiss des Rothirsches' (Research into dentition of red deer), *Forstwirtschaft und Forstwissenschaft* (Hanover, 1939)

4 Meyer, W. 'Zur Herstellung von Verbissmitteln' (Towards manufacturing of anti-browsing deterrents), *Seifensiederzeitung* (1939)

5 Red Deer Commission. Newsletters, HMSO
———. Annual Reports, HMSO

6 Nature Conservancy. Range Ecology Research—1st Report (1970)

7 Müller, F. Unpublished lectures: Dept of Forestry and Game, University of Eberswalde (1967)

8 Ueckerman, E. *Wildstandbewirtschaftung und Wildschadenhuttung beim Rehwild* (Management and damage control with roe) (Neuwid, 1957)

9 Mottl, S. *Bonitace houbiště zvěři srnči* (Case against damage by deer) (Czechoslovak Government Publication, 1954)
———. *Potrava srnči zvěři* (Feeding of deer) (Biologia, Prague, 1957)

10 Ueckerman, E. *Das Damwild* (Fallow Deer) (Hamburg, 1956)

11 De Nahlik, A. J. *Wild Deer* (London, 1958)

12 Dziegielewski, S. *Jelen* (Red deer) (Warsaw, 1970)

13 Pielowski, Z. *Sarna* (Roe deer) (Warsaw, 1970)

References

14 Miszewski, H. (ed). *Przewodnik-Informator Lowiecki* (Guide and Handbook for shooting sportsmen) (Warsaw, 1955).

15 Paslawski, T. *Lowiectwo* (Game shooting) (Warsaw, 1971)

16 Turke, F. *Mittel gegen Wildschaden und ihre Anwendung* (Game damage remedies and their usage) (Munich, 1952)

——. *Mittel gegen Wildschaden richtig Anwenden* (Proper usage of game prevention remedies) (Munich, 1957)

17 Highlands and Islands Development Board and Rowett Research Institute (ed Bannerman, M. M., and Blaxter, K. L.). *The Husbanding of Red Deer* (Aberdeen, 1969)

18 Bubenik, A. *Das Geweih* (Antlers) (Hamburg, 1966)

19 Nature Conservancy. *Red Deer Research in Scotland*, Progress Report No 1 (1967)

20 The Game Conservancy. *Forestry and Game*, Proceedings of a symposium (1971)

INDEX

age distribution, 145, 146, 204, 215
age recognition, 41; by body, 42; by tooth formation, 53
antler as asset, 164, 165
antler development characteristics, 62; in the crown, 71; in fallow deer, 80 et seq; in the general shape, 63, 70; in old animals, 73; in red deer, 67; related to age, 64 et seq; in roe deer, 74 et seq
antler evaluation, 165; CIC method, 170–4; non–CIC methods, 175; red deer, 170
antlers: cleaning, 35; damage to, 33; development connected with sex, 35, 37; growth of, 33; heredity characteristics, 35; shedding of, 35
archaeological findings, 21

background to management, 139
biological area, 139; capacity, 140; competition with other animals, 140
body build, 42; development, 44

calf, 39; marking, 41; mortality, 40; shooting, 168–9, 199, 206 et seq, 228 et seq
calving rate, 143
capacity of area, 140, 157, 204, 230

categorisation of land, 122
classification: red deer, 146 et seq, 210; roe deer, 147–8
coat changing, 46, 50
composition of herds, 147
conservation, 161
co-operation, 150 et seq, 183
cover, need for, 25
cropping age, 213
counting: at feeding places, 94; by observation, 93; dead beasts found, 96; in forests, 94; methods, 91 et seq; reasons for, 91, 93; recording of, 92, 94; related to culling, 93; reports, 94, 95; timing of, 91, 92; use of radio when, 92
culling: red deer, 146, 147, 206; roe deer, 147, 148

damage, 97; basic considerations, 98; to body, effects, 33; by other animals, 97; categorisation of prevention, 100; control, 99, 103, 189 et seq; in the field, 101; in the woodland, 102, 107, 119; related to values, 99, 113, 120, 184, 186; relation to feeding, 101, 129; population, 100, 103, 117, 118
damage, prevention of, 104, 109; by chemicals, 113, 189 et seq; by home-made compounds,

damage, prevention—*cont.*
112; by taste repellents, 113;
by toxity of deterrents, 112
deer: adaptation to environment,
26; as asset, 212 et seq, 219; as
conservation problem, 161; as
economic product, 180 et seq,
203 et seq, 219 et seq; as profit
centre, 161; by-products, 163,
164, 237; calf and fawn, 39;
development potential, 178;
early (Norman) laws, 22;
habitat, 25; herd, 30; in history,
21; in parks, 27; psychology
and behaviour, 28, 162; repellents, 189; rut, 26, 30;
spreading of, 165
deer management: with other
animals, 181; for profit, 161,
164; for venison, 181; objectives, 162, 165, 181, 204;
standards, 154 et seq; studies,
161
density, 119, 141; establishment
of figures, 120 et seq, 141; in
various environments, 121;
state in Scotland, 118; studies
of, 118
digestive process, 132
dormant gestation, 39

early deer laws, 22, 24
economic considerations of roe
deer damage, 184
economics of deer, 157, 161 et
seq, 182 et seq, 237 et seq

fawn, 39
feeding: capacity of land, 140,
157, 182; changes in, result of,
125; chemical components

needed, 129, 193 et seq; compounds, 139; fields, 137; guide
lines from Schneeberg, 127;
habits in, 27, 162; influence on
antlers, 126, 127; methods,
136; needs, 127, 128; of deer,
27, 101, 125, 130, 183; related
to damage, 129; requirements
related to weight, 141; values,
121, 193 et seq
female deer, age grouping, 46
field damage, 101
food: additives, 125, 127, 136;
as limiting factor of quality,
157; conversion, 131, 132; conversion during antler building,
135
forest: dependance of one upon
another, 153, 157; single-sex,
153

game management, 161
gestation, 39

habitat, 25
habits, roe deer, 31
heat, 38
herd, 28, 30, 141, 147; constitution of, 143, 144, 147
hierarchical structure, roe buck,
32
hind: culling, 47, 48, 144 et seq,
203 et seq; forests, 153; signs
of poor condition in, 48
Hoffman pyramid, 142, 144, 198
et seq, 207 et seq

incisors as means of age recognition, 56

jaw malformation, 56

land: capacity, 140, 157, 182, 203, 230; improvements, 157; sharing with other interests, 182, 239 et seq
late rut, 39
leading hind, 28, 48
life cycle: of fallow deer, 51; of red deer, 49; of roe deer, 52

management: approach to, 154, 223 et seq; objectives of, 154, 181, 183, 204, 219; overheads, 180; planned, 139, 212 et seq, 219 et seq, 228 et seq; standards, 154, 155
marking of calves, 41
metabolism, 132
molars, age recognition by, 57 et seq

park deer, 27
planned management, 139, 186, 203 et seq; shooting, 27, 143, 145, 167, 205, 228 et seq
predators, 140, 142
prehistoric records, 21
psychology of deer, 28

quality of animals, 155; of recording during counts, 93

recognition by body build, 42, 214; by tooth formation, 57
red deer: evaluation of antler, 121; habits, 28
reproductive cycle: female, 38 et seq; male, 33 et seq
roe deer: age structure, 147, 148; as asset, 165; doe development, 50; doe dormant gestation, 39; habits, 31; rings, 38; territory, 32

rumen, 132, 135
rut, 26, 30, 36, 142, 167; fallow deer, 37; red deer, 36, 142; roe deer, 37, 142

seasonal movement of deer, 153
selective shooting, 125 et seq; error in, 154; programme, 167; stags, hinds, calves, 168, 169, 206
sex ratio, 125, 142, 203 et seq, 215, 219 et seq, 226, 228 et seq; and shooting plan, 143; natural, 142 et seq
sexual maturity, 36
shedding of antlers, 35
shelter, need for, 125
shooting plan, 27, 143, 167, 205, 228 et seq; Hoffman pyramid, 198, 206; related to sex ratio, 143, 144, 228; return from, 185
shooting policy, 150, 154
single-sex forest, 150
stag forest, 153
stalking, evaluation of, 167 et seq, 186; evaluation of fees of, 170, 220; grounds, 172; revenue from, 198, 212 et seq, 226

territorial possessiveness, roe deer, 32, 37
tooth formation, 53; changes in, table of, 60, 61; incisors, 56, 58; molars, 57; register as aid to age recognition, 58
tree protection against damage, 105
twins, 39

urea, 132
utilisation of land, 156, 239 et seq

velvet, 25, 35
venison: preference for ore, 165;
production, 212; value, 165

woodland: as feeding potential,
120; damage to, 102, 107, 119;
potential as deer holding, 185